D1179175

The Colonel's Cookbook

The Colonel's Cookbook

**Douglas Sutherland
with Diana Sutherland
and Wendy Hartman**

FREDERICK MULLER LIMITED
LONDON

First published in Great Britain 1980 by Frederick Muller
Limited, London, NW2 6LE

British Library Cataloguing in Publication Data
Sutherland, Douglas, b.1919
    The colonel's cookbook.
    1. Cookery, English
    I. Title   II. Sutherland, Diana
    III. Hartman, Wendy
    641.5'942   TX717

ISBN 0–584–10373–5

Printed in Great Britain by Biddles Ltd., Guildford, Surrey

Contents

Introduction

The author of this book has resisted all efforts to persuade him to publish it under his own name. This is largely because he does not wish, at his advanced age, to contend with the fame which the work would undoubtedly thrust upon him; but it must also be said that the Colonel is an intuitive cook whose methods are based more on instinct than on rules. He was never one for exact measurements in pounds and pints, even less in grammes and litres. The editors have therefore used his own notes and instructions but, in deference to the scientific age in which we live – removed, it would seem, by a million light years, from the age in which the Colonel was reared – added those details regarding heat, weight, time, etc., which are *de rigeur* in cookery books today. They have also tested and, in some cases, modified, all the Colonel's recipes, a task in which the invaluable assistance of Diana Sutherland must not go unrecorded.

It seems appropriate to start by describing the author's distinguished career, if only to satisfy the reader of his qualifications for the task. He was born at the beginning of this century, the second son of a Scottish landowning family with a long tradition of service to the Empire. He was brought up in the family mansion, which consisted of forty-five unheated rooms. There was a small army of servants, the most senior of whom were paid as much as £15 per annum and had a whole day's holiday every year, but who were pampered to the extent that they were not required to eat salmon or venison more than twice a week. No such consideration was shown to the members of the family, who subsisted on an

1

exclusive diet of whatever game or fish was in season. Far from turning him for life against what are now considered to be luxury foods, it infected him with a desire to prove that there were ways of preparing these foods which did not render them entirely tasteless.

The warmest room in the house was the kitchen with its vast cooking range so, when his parents were away from home, which was frequently, he spent much of his time there, democractically sharing the servants' meals. In this way he learned to appreciate such dishes as home-made soups, stovies, herrings in oatmeal, and haggis.

He was educated at one of our leading public schools, where the staple diet was a watery stew and rice pudding, and the last meal of the day consisted of unsweetened cocoa with a thick slice of bread and margarine. This experience served to steel him in his resolve to fare better in later life.

While his elder brother was groomed to take over the running of the family estates, he, following the unbreakable family tradition, was sent into the Regular Army and was almost immediately posted to France. It was here that he laid the foundations of his distinguished military career. On a diet of bully beef and plum and apple jam he won the Military Cross at the second Battle of the Somme and was later awarded the French Croix de Guerre.

After the signing of the Armistice he volunteered for service with the Indian Army and spent the next eighteen years in such well-known stations as Poona and Pondicherry, with occasional tours of duty to the North-West Frontier. It was during this period that his true genius as a cook came into flower.

It is true to say that no man can reach complete fulfilment in his career without an element of luck. In the case of the Colonel it was his great good fortune to have 'Jumbo' Wodderspoon as his Commanding Officer. 'Jumbo', who put his not inconsiderable stomach before all else, was quick to discover the author's interest in cooking and gave him every encouragement. Instead of requiring him to turn out daily for polo practice, his C.O. allowed him to spend his spare time wandering through the native bazaars in search of new and more pungent spices with which to flavour his dishes. Soon he became familiar with Jawstrie and Khush-Khush, Undruck and Nareul and many other aids to the production of more and more tasty creations. He rose early, to buy the freshest meat, fish and game before they started to putrefy in the midday sun; he supervised the activities of the Officers' Mess cooks, whether Hindu or Moslem, down to the smallest detail.

It was not long before 'Jumbo' Wodderspoon could boast that he kept the finest table in the whole of the Indian Army and there were few Generals who could resist his invitations to dinner. It was inevitable that this should result in his early promotion to command a brigade. With equal inevitability he took the author with him, promoting him to the rank of Captain and making him President of the Brigade Mess Committee.

From this moment his future was never in doubt. By the time it came for him to retire, he was a full Colonel, and Catering Adviser to Government House, devising delicious and unusual meals for the many distinguished visitors who sat down at the Viceroy's table.

On his return to England his interest in cooking took on a fresh lease of life. Whole new vistas opened up for him with the availability of the excellent meat, fish and fowl of the Home Country. He took a modest house in Hampshire, where he became an enthusiastic gardener, growing his own vegetables and experimenting with a host of new dishes which the hot climate of India had denied him in the past. For the first time he began to regret his years of service abroad.

With the outbreak of the Second World War the War Office found a ready use for him as a senior officer in the Catering Corps but the job gave him little satisfaction. His real metier was in carefully prepared individual dishes and the vast tonnage of spam and other foods with which he was required to concern himself did little to satisfy his creative instincts. To relieve the monotony he got married, late in life, to a Colonel in the A.T.S.

His elder brother having died without issue, he inherited the family seat in Scotland and retired there gratefully at the end of the hostilities. Unable to obtain or afford servants, he and his mem-sahib live in discomfort in part of one wing where the only modern room is a well-equipped kitchen.

Fortunately his wife shows no interest at all in cooking, devoting her time to being President of the local W.V.S. and Captain of the Golf Club. The lack of female interference in culinary matters suits the Colonel perfectly. As he once remarked, 'A woman's place is in bed. She should only be allowed up to get in the coals'.

If rendered somewhat irascible by the rapidly spiralling cost of living and especially the price of whisky, he is living out a contented old age, grinding his spices in his *hummum dusta* with his *humundusta ke duntee* (which he cannot understand his wife calling a pestle and mortar) and giving occasional dinner parties for his neighbours, who talk about nothing else for days afterwards.

This book is a distillation of his wisdom gained over a lifetime of experience.

DOUGLAS SUTHERLAND
DIANA SUTHERLAND   WENDY HARTMAN

Preface by the Colonel

From time to time friends of mine, knowing my interest in cooking, send me cookery books as presents and I am horrified to see how few of them pay attention to the preparation of good British food, which is without doubt the finest in the world. Continental meat is dreadful by British standards, their game lacks variety, and their fish is not always of the highest standard.

The criterion of a good dish is that it should stand on its own merits and not have to rely on some rich and difficult sauce to give it flavour. Nor does it have to be expensive. A man can dine like a king off a couple of herring fresh from the North Sea, if they are prepared correctly.

There is also a sort of snobbery which has crept into our culinary vocabulary. Does the 'faggot of herbs' grown since time immemorial in British gardens, perhaps not have the same posh sound as a *bouquet garni*?

I do not subscribe to the view that the British are worse cooks than their Continental counterparts, but it may be that they are brainwashed into a belief that their native foods have to be prepared according to some exotic recipe to make them edible. The result, regrettably, is often disastrous.

I have not excluded any recipes from this book because the ingredients are expensive; nor have I disdained to include any which are cheap and easy to prepare, but I have borne in mind that most hostesses today are their own cooks and bottlewashers and do not want to spend more time than they must in the kitchen when they should be attending to their guests.

I may be criticized for omitting some classic dishes, but I make no apology. My aim is simply to make some of our well-known dishes taste better and introduce some original recipes which I have seen described nowhere else.

A final word about quantities. Remember that – except for baking – cooking is not an exact science. The quantities have been supplied by my editors as a guide and can be varied to taste. A bachelor acquaintance of mine who fends for himself with the aid of cookery books invariably doubles the ingredients he likes and halves those he does not care for and assures me that the results are highly satisfactory. Most of the recipes in this book are for from 4 to 6 people but only you know how hungry, or greedy, your friends are.

Soups

Soups

Some of the best soups are inspirational. That is to say, by the use of a combination of leftovers you suddenly produce a really memorable soup without being able to remember exactly what you did.

The same thing applies to the good cook's standby – stock soup. It is really extraordinary in these days, when good husbandry is of increasing importance, that the housewife relies more and more on tinned or packaged soups which do not even have the virtue of being palatable, whilst a good stock soup is easy to make, economical and tasty.

In the old days even the most elaborate soups were inexpensive to make. Nowadays many of the old specialities are priced out of existence, like the following which I came across in our old household recipe book:–

'Put six oysters for each person and one tablespoon of white stock into an earthenware pot. Stew gently until all the liquid of the oysters is extracted. Season with salt. Throw away the oysters and add two fresh oysters for each person. Serve very hot in cups and just before serving add a desertspoonful of shipped cream on the top of the broth in each cup.'

On the other hand, there are many delicious and reasonably economical soups which can be served at a dinner party. Here are a few ideas:

How to Make and Keep your Stock Pot:

If you want a rich brown stock which is ideal for flavouring stews and sauces, you will need to buy some boiling beef and simmer it gently in a large pot to which water should be added. The quantity of water is usually 1 quart (1¼ litres) of water to each pound (500 g) of meat, but you may need less if the pot has a close-fitting lid.

First bring the stock to the boil, remove any scum that appears and simmer until the stock has been reduced by half – then, and only then, should the vegetables be added, cut in large pieces. Allow to each 4 quarts (5 litres) of water – 1 onion; 1 carrot; ½ turnip; a stick of celery; salt; 12 peppercorns. Do not use ground pepper as it makes the stock cloudy.

A more basic stock pot is made simply by boiling up bones and water for three or four hours. This should be boiled up every day and fresh water added as needed, together with any marrow bones. Neither fat nor green vegetables should ever be put into a stock pot as it makes it sour. Every two or three days the meat from which the goodness has been taken should be removed.

GAME SOUP

Should a well-meaning friend send you a game bird – be it grouse, partridge or pheasant – which has either been so badly shot or is so old as to be an insult to your guests, here is a recipe for making it into very palatable soup.

1 game bird: either pheasant, grouse or partridge	2 sticks celery
1 quart (1¼ litres) good stock	2 oz (50 g) coarse oatmeal
1 teaspoon salt	¼ pint (150 ml) stock
6 peppercorns	1 tablespoon red wine *or*
6 juniper berries (optional)	1 tablespoon single cream

Slightly under-roast the bird and remove all the flesh. Leave the breast on one side and pound the remaining meat in a mortar. Put the bones in a pan with the quart (1¼ litres) of stock, bring to the boil and skim. Add salt, black peppercorns and juniper berries, if liked. Add celery and simmer for two hours. Then strain. Make a cream by gently frying the oatmeal in butter, gradually adding the remaining ¼ pint (150 ml) stock. Away from the heat stir into the rest of the stock, add the pounded flesh of the bird, and simmer for 20 minutes more. Dice the breast fillet, fry gently in a little butter and add to the soup, together with a tablespoon of red wine, or cream if preferred.

POTATO AND LEEK SOUP

12 medium sized
   potatoes (sliced)
6 leeks (chopped)
1 marrow bone
2 sticks of celery
   (chopped)

½ cup of pearl barley
3 pints (1¾ litres) water
1 dessert spoon salt
black pepper to taste

Put all the ingredients into a large pot and simmer gently on the stove for an hour, by which time the potatoes will have cooked and will have added a thickening basis to the soup.

WINDSOR SOUP

Beware of a dreadful offering described as Brown Windsor Soup which seems to consist of a beef cube dissolved in hot water. I don't know if the following recipe is as served to the Royal Family, but it is a very different proposition.

1 pint (600 ml) good
   stock
a little macaroni cut
   about ½ inch (25 cm)
   in length

4 yolks of eggs
¼ pint (150 ml) cream

Put the stock and the macaroni on and bring to the boil. A few minutes before serving pour on to the previously blended yolks of eggs and cream. Stir over the heat until hot but do not boil again or it will curdle. Serve with croutons of fried bread.

SPINACH SOUP

8 oz (225 g) packet frozen
   spinach
1½ oz (35 g) butter
1½ (35 g) plain flour

½ pint (300 ml) milk
3½ oz (75 g) carton
   single cream
salt and pepper

Cook the spinach according to the instructions on the packet, strain and reserve the liquid. Make the liquid up to 1 pint (600 ml) with some water. Melt the butter, stir in the flour and cook gently for a few minutes. Gradually stir in the hot liquid and milk and bring to the boil, stirring all the time. Add the spinach, simmer for 3 minutes and push through a sieve or liquidize. Add the single cream, season to taste and serve hot.

COCK – A – LEEKIE

1 boiling fowl or some
   jointed pieces
6 leeks
2 quarts (2½ litres)
   chicken stock

1 tablespoon salt
1 teaspoon black pepper
12 prunes, soaked
   overnight in cold tea

Take two or three joints of a boiling fowl, or the whole bird if you have it, and put into a large saucepan with three of the leeks, well washed and chopped, and the stock. Bring to the boil and simmer for two hours until the bird is tender. Remove from the pan and clean off grease with absorbent paper. Cut the chicken into neat pieces. Return to the pan with the remainder of the leeks, cut into 1 inch (2.5 cm) lengths, the strained prunes and the salt and pepper. Simmer gently until leeks and prunes are tender, about 15 – 20 minutes, and serve.

13

SKINK SOUP

Zoologists will know that the skink is a small lizard. Do not be put off this delicious soup, which is the speciality of a small fishing port, Cullen, in the north of Scotland, and has nothing to do with lizards. I don't know how it got its odd name.

1 finnan-haddock	seasoning
1 pint (600 ml) water	4 tablespoons mashed
1 chopped onion	potato
1 pint (600 ml) milk	2 ozs (50 g) butter

Put the haddock in a pan with enough water to cover. Bring to the boil, add the onion and simmer for about 15 minutes. Remove haddock, and skin, bone and flake the fish. Return the skin and bones to the stock, simmer for one hour and then strain the stock. Boil a pint (600 ml) of milk separately and add the stock with the flaked fish and seasoning. Simmer for a few minutes and then whisk in enough potato to make the soup a nice consistency. Add butter and pepper to taste.

HARE SOUP

1 hare	1 carrot
1½ oz (35 g) butter	3 onions
1½ oz (35 g) flour	salt and pepper

Skin a hare, collect the blood and mix well with water until you have about 5 pints (3 litres) of liquid. Melt the butter in a large pan and stir in the flour, cooking gently for one minute. Strain the liquid and pour onto the butter and flour mixture, stirring carefully until it comes to the boil. Skim. Add the hare, cut in pieces,· a carrot and three onions. Simmer very slowly for 3½ hours, skimming when necessary. Pour through a hair sieve, skim again, season with salt and pepper and serve.

MULLIGATAWNY SOUP

1 rabbit	2 tablespoons curry powder
6 onions	
1 carrot	1 oz (25 g) butter
1 turnip	1 oz (25 g) flour
salt to taste	a little sherry or Marsala if liked
some bones from the butcher	

Joint the rabbit and simmer in water with the vegetables until tender, about 1 hour. Remove all the meat and put into a basin. Put the gravy bones into the water in which the rabbit was boiled and simmer for a couple of hours, then strain. Return the liquid to the saucepan. Fry the curry powder in the butter for a few minutes, add the flour and cook gently for a further minute, stirring constantly. Gradually stir in about ½ pint (300 ml) hot stock, return to saucepan and boil for 15 minutes. Add rabbit, heat thoroughly, season and serve. In the opinion of many this soup is much improved by the addition of sherry or Marsala.

RICH HARE SOUP

One large hare
½ lb (225 g) bacon
4 pints (2½ litres) stock
2 onions
a blade of mace
1 bayleaf
a bunch of herbs: thyme,
    parsley and marjoram
6 peppercorns

½ turnip
3 carrots
1 stick celery
½ lb (225 g) fresh
    breadcrumbs
1 large glass of port or
    red wine
1½ teaspoons salt

Cut the hare into small joints and the bacon into slices. Put the hare into a pan with the bacon, stock, onions, mace, herbs and peppercorns and simmer for about 2½ hours. Remove the bacon and pound in a mortar and then take out the hare, cutting some of the meat from the back and legs – keep all of this on one side. Remove the bayleaf and peppercorns and put the remaining vegetables through the liquidizer. Put this back into the stewpan, together with the pounded bacon and breadcrumbs. Now add the cut-up meat and port or wine and simmer again for ½ an hour. Season to taste and serve very hot, but do not let it boil.

SCOTCH BROTH

A piece of boiling beef
salt
3 diced carrots
2 sliced leeks

½ diced turnip
8 ozs (225 g) split peas
4 ozs (125 g) pearl barley

Put 7 pints (4 litres) of water in a saucepan and bring to the boil – then add the boiling beef, salt to taste, and the vegetables and barley. Simmer for about three hours and serve piping hot.

Fish

Fish

The window of a good fish shop used to be a delight, with its great variety of fish from the everyday to the exotic spread out before one. Alas, this is just another of the good things of life which we once took for granted and which are now gone, never to return.

The lordly turbot and the great halibut are seldom seen. Even commonplace fish like skate and the delicate little dabs seem to have disappeared, whilst luxuries like lobster, crab and oysters are far beyond the reach of all but the very rich.

Take care when you are buying fish that what you are getting is really fresh. I personally refrain from buying fish on a Monday as it is likely that it has not been freshly landed. Generally speaking, it is easy to tell fish which are not completely fresh from the dullness of their scales and the lacklustre glaze of their eyes. In particular, fish like herring and mackerel defy the arts of the most skilful chef if they are not completely fresh.

If, for a special occasion, you decide to invest in a salmon, be sure to choose the most silvery one you can. If the fish is coloured, it means it has been in fresh water too long and is good for nothing but smoking. The surest sign of a fresh fish is if you can spot sea lice still clinging to the body. If you can get them, sea trout are much less expensive and, to my mind, among the finest fish available.

Like good meat, do not mess around with game fish like salmon, sea trout and brown trout. Personally I never serve any of them with anything but melted butter. Salmon, for some people the king of fish, is seldom well cooked. It is so easy to make it dry and unpalatable. I have found this simple recipe infallible.

Poached Salmon:

Fill a large pan, or ideally a fish kettle, with water to which vinegar, a bay leaf, an onion, chopped carrots, fennel, if available, and seasoning are added. Put the fish in whole so that it is covered by water and bring to the boil – boil for *three minutes only* and then leave in the water until cold. Remove, skin, and place on a dish and garnish with cucumber.

Trout:

Try to obtain brown brook trout – the best size is about three to a pound (or around 200g each).

In general, the bigger the trout, especially Rainbow trout, the less sweet they are.

To cook, simply clean and cut off the head. Then grill, liberally larded with butter and seasoned, for 5–10 minutes depending on size.

Herrings In Oatmeal:

Clean and wipe the herrings with a damp cloth, coat in medium or coarse oatmeal and fry for a couple of minutes each side until cooked through.

Serve with mustard or horseradish sauce.

HADDOCK CASSEROLE

1½ lb (675 g) fresh
  haddock
4oz (100 g) crab or
  prawns
2 small onions, chopped
2 oz (50 g) mushrooms,
  sliced

2 oz (50 g) butter
1 oz (25 g) flour
1 15 oz (415 ml) can
  tomato juice
1 pinch mixed herbs
2 teaspoons sugar
salt and pepper

Wash fish, cut in pieces and put in a greased fireproof dish. Fry onions and mushrooms in butter, add flour when they begin to colour and stir continuously for two minutes. Gradually add the previously heated tomato juice and bring to the boil, then add the herbs, seasoning and sugar and pour over the fish. Cover with greased paper and cook in a moderate oven (350°F, 180°C, Gas Mark 4) for half an hour.

HADDOCK AND SHRIMP MOUSSE

1½ lb (675 g) filleted
  haddock
4 oz (100 g) peeled
  prawns or shrimps
3 oz (75 g) chopped
  mushrooms
4 oz (100 g) flour
1½ oz (40 g) butter

¾ pint (400 ml) double
  cream
¾ pint (400 ml) milk
2 eggs
2 small glasses sherry
1 tablespoon tomato
  puree
salt
pepper

Grease a large charlotte mould or round cake tin. Skin fish, cut into pieces and mince finely. Cover and chill for half an hour. Melt butter, stir in half the flour and a pinch of salt. Cook for one minute, stirring all the time. Away from the heat, blend in ¼ of the cream and all the milk, both previously heated. Return to the heat and cook for one minute, stirring continuously. Remove from the heat and beat in egg yolks, half the sherry and the tomato puree. Return to the heat and stir in the prawns and mushrooms. Cook for one minute and set aside.

Mix the rest of the flour with the haddock and seasoning. Fold in the beaten egg whites and remainder of the cream, whipped, then fold ²/₃ of this round the inside of the mould. Fill with ²/₃ of the prawn mixture. Cover mould with remaining fish mixture. Cover with greased paper and place in a roasting tin. Add two inches (5 cm) of boiling water and bake at 325°F, 170°C, Gas Mark 3, for 1¾ – 2 hours. Turn out, and serve hot or cold with the remains of the prawn mixture and sherry as a sauce.

CREAM OF HADDOCK

1 lb (450 g) fresh
    haddock fillet
1 pint (600 ml) milk
1 pint (600 ml) water
2 onions
pinch of thyme

seasoning to taste
6 oz (150 g) butter
2 oz (50 g) Parmesan
    cheese
½ cup stale breadcrumbs

Put milk and water into a saucepan with one onion, thyme, pepper and salt. Simmer for half an hour, put in the fish and continue simmering until tender, (about 15 minutes). Soften a chopped onion in 2 oz (50 g) of the butter, stir in the flour and cook, still stirring for one or two minutes. Gradually blend in one pint (600 ml) of the strained cooking liquid and cook a few minutes more. Check seasoning, and add 1 oz (25 g) of the Parmesan cheese. Skin and flake the fish and fold into the sauce. Butter a good deep dish and turn fish into it. Dot surface with remaining butter and sprinkle with breadcrumbs and Parmesan cheese. Bake lightly until brown and serve.

FISH AND BACON CHOWDER

1 lb (450 g) fish, white or
    yellow
1 large onion
1 lb (450 g) potatoes

6 bacon rashers
1 pint (600 ml) milk
salt and pepper

Butter casserole dish and set aside. Wash and cut up fish, peel and slice onion and potatoes. Rind and cut up the bacon and fry lightly. Put a layer of bacon in a casserole, next a layer of fish, then onion and potatoes. Season well and continue until the ingredients are all used up, finishing with a layer of potato. Add milk to cover by about an inch and bake in a fairly hot oven, (375°F, 190°C, Gas Mark 5), for about an hour, or until cooked.

FISH PIE

1½ lb (675 g) cod fillet
1 pint (600 ml) milk
2 oz (50 g) flour
2 oz (50 g) butter
2 hard-boiled eggs

2 lb (900 g) potatoes,
    mashed with butter,
    milk and seasoning
seasoning
chopped parsley
grated cheese

Simmer the cod in milk until cooked, about 15 minutes. Make a white sauce with the butter, flour and the milk the

25

fish was cooked in. (See page 34). Season and add parsley. Fold the flaked fish into the sauce, together with the chopped, hard-boiled eggs and put in a casserole. Cover with the mashed potatoes and dot with butter and grated cheese. Put in a hot oven, (400°F, 200°C, Gas Mark 6), to brown and heat through for 20 minutes.

FISH CREAM

6 oz (175 g) fillet of
    white fish
2 oz (50 g) fresh
    breadcrumbs
½ a cup of milk

1 oz (25 g) butter
2 eggs
1 tablespoon of single
    cream
salt and pepper

Put the breadcrumbs in a basin, soak with warm milk and a small piece of butter. Rub fish through a sieve, add to the breadcrumbs, beat in the eggs, then the cream. Season. Put in a buttered bowl and steam for half an hour. (For steaming instructions see recipe on page 85).

SHRIMP PIE

1½ pints (900 ml)
    shrimps or prawns
2 slices stale bread
2 glasses white wine
1 blade mace
¼ of a ground nutmeg
pinch of thyme
tablespoon of parsley

salt and pepper
cayenne pepper
2 oz (50 g) butter
5 tomatoes
1 stick of celery
1 bayleaf
½ pint (300 ml) fish
    stock

Shell shrimps and use shells for making stock. Remove crust from the bread and grate it finely. Moisten remaining bread with the white wine, season with mace, nutmeg, thyme, parsley, salt and cayenne pepper and then mix thoroughly with $^2/_3$ of the shrimps. Put in a pie dish, sprinkle with the grated crust, dot with butter and bake till lightly browned. Serve with the sauce handed separately.

For the Sauce:
Take remaining shrimps, put in a saucepan with the tomatoes, skinned and finely chopped, chopped celery, bayleaf, pinch of thyme and parsley. Mix well and cook for a few minutes. Season with salt, pepper and cayenne pepper and add ½ a pint (300 ml) of fish stock and cook for a few minutes longer.

COD CUTLETS

4 cod cutlets, 1½″ (4 cm) thick	½ teacup dried breadcrumbs
6 cloves of garlic	1 hard-boiled egg
2 teaspoons turmeric	½ pint (300 ml) milk
tabasco sauce	1 oz (25 g) butter
1 cup cooking oil	1 oz (25 g) flour

Crush garlic and mix with turmeric and a few drops of tabasco, adding a little oil to bind it. Spread mixture on both sides of cod cutlets pressed well in and stand for one hour.

Cover with breadcrumbs on both sides and fry in the remainder of the oil. Serve with a hard-boiled egg chopped up in a white sauce made with ½ pint (300 ml) milk, 1 oz (25 g) butter and 1 oz (25 g) flour. (See page 34).

COD WITH SWEET RED PEPPERS AND TOMATOES

1½ – 2 lb (675 g – 900
   g) cod
3–4 tablespoons oil
2 lb (900 g) chopped
   onion
2–3 sliced sweet red
   peppers
flour

5–6 tomatoes
chopped parsley
garlic
1 bayleaf
1 small glass of white
   wine
salt and pepper

Cut fish into ¾" (2 cm) thick slices, then cut in half and remove the bone. Heat the oil in a sauté pan, add onion and peppers and cook gently until the onion is soft but not brown. Season fish, coat with flour and put in pan. Cook slowly and slightly, then turn fish and add tomatoes, peeled, seeded and chopped, together with the parsley, garlic, bayleaf and wine.
   Cover and cook for 12–15 minutes.
   Serve with fresh boiled potatoes.

FILLET OF SOLE IN LEMON PARSLEY BUTTER

2 lb (900 g) fillets of sole
½ cup butter
2 tablespoons cornflour
3 tablespoons lemon juice

1 tablespoon chopped
   parsley
celery salt
pepper

Melt butter, add cornflour, lemon juice and parsley and blend well. Dip each fillet in sauce. Place in a well buttered baking dish or casserole. Sprinkle with celery salt and pepper, cover and cook in the oven for about half an hour. (350°F, 180°C, Gas Mark 4.)

POACHED SOLE WITH ONIONS AND TOMATOES

For two people

2 sole	juice of ½ lemon
1 small onion, finely chopped	2 tomatoes
desertspoon chopped parsley	1 tablespoon butter
	aubergine for garnish
3 tablespoons water	seasoned flour
3 tablespoons white wine	oil
	salt and pepper

Butter a shallow fireproof dish wide enough to lay the fish side by side, and put onion and parsley in the bottom. Lay sole on top, add water, wine and lemon juice. Add tomatoes, peeled, chopped and seeded, and seasonings. Bring slowly to the boil on top of the stove, cover and cook in a moderate oven (350°F, 180°C, Gas Mark 4) for 15–20 minutes. Put sole into a serving dish, stir butter into liquor left and pour over the fish. Garnish with slices of aubergine, dipped in seasoned flour and fried in oil.

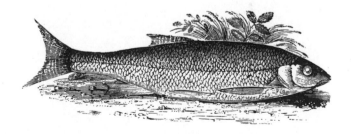

Poultry

Poultry

Hints on Cooking Poultry

To Cook very young Chickens:

Coat each bird in plenty of butter and roast, basting well, in the oven at 400°F, 200°C, Gas Mark 6, for about 20 minutes.

Remove and cut birds into halves and rub over each with the yolk of two eggs. Roll in breadcrumbs and fry for 5 minutes on each side in hot butter.

Serve very hot.

CHICKEN WITH TOMATOES & ONIONS

1 farm chicken	stock
1 large tin tomatoes	¼ lb (100 g) mushrooms
2 large onions	1 tablespoon seasoning

Put your chicken in a deep stewpan with a lid and pour on the tomatoes and sliced onions. Add the chicken stock, mushrooms and seasoning. Bring to the boil on the top of the stove, cover and place in a slow oven (325°F, 170°C, Gas Mark 3) for 2 hours. If necessary, reduce the liquid by boiling over a quick flame. Serve with rice.

CHICKEN LEFTOVER

Chicken pieces (cooked)
chicken stock
¼ pint (150 ml) double
    cream
dessertspoon
    Worcestershire Sauce

½ teaspoon made
    English Mustard
dessertspoon Soya Sauce
½ teaspoon French
    Mustard

Place the pieces of chicken in a fireproof serving dish, pour a little hot stock over them, cover and place in a moderately hot oven (400°F, 200°C, Gas Mark 5) for 15 minutes or until heated through.

In the meantime make the sauce. Whip the cream until thick and then beat in the rest of the ingredients. When the chicken is heated through remove from the oven, strain off the stock and pour the sauce over the chicken. Put back in the oven for 5 or 10 minutes before serving.

WHITE SAUCE *(to go with chicken)*

2 oz (50 g) butter or
    margarine

1 pint (600 ml
2 oz (50 g) flour

This is the basic white sauce and can be varied in consistency by adjusting the ingredients.

Melt the butter in a saucepan and add the flour. Cook carefully together for a few minutes, stirring constantly, but do not brown. Add the previously heated milk gradually and continue stirring to prevent lumps forming. Bring to the boil and simmer gently for 5 minutes to cook the flour, then add whatever flavouring and seasoning is required. Strain through a sieve to ensure a smooth, lumpless consistency.

Turkey

Turkey can either be quite delicious or completely inedible, according to the way in which it is cooked.

The main trouble in cooking a turkey is that if you stuff it with the traditional oatmeal and onion (see below) or even forcemeat, however much care you take with basting the bird, the stuffing draws the natural juices out of the body of the bird, which results in it becoming dry and tasteless.

Instead, try making a fresh fruit salad (fresh oranges, apple, banana, grapes, etc.) and stuff the bird at both ends. The juices of the fruit salad will permeate the meat, making it both moist and of a delicate flavour. You can then slow roast the bird for 20 minutes a lb (450 g) at 325°F, 170°C, Gas Mark 3.

Some experts prefer to stuff the bird with cheap steak, which has a similar effect. Do not try to eat the steak afterwards. It will however, be much appreciated by your dog.

Make your stuffing separately as follows:–

OATMEAL & ONION STUFFING

½ lb (225 g) oatmeal
2 onions (chopped fine)
enough water to make a
    doughy consistency

1 teaspoon salt
pinch of black pepper

Place oatmeal in a bowl and add the chopped onions and seasoning, then bind together with the water.

Game

Game

Opinions on which is the best game bird in the kitchen are as varied and as hotly discussed among epicures as such knotty questions as who was the best batsman ever to play for England are debated among cricket fans.

My father was a great lover of game with one exception – the capercaillie. This, the largest and most handsome of all our indigenous game birds, was common in his youth and after a period of near extinction is now becoming common again, so his recipe for cooking it may be worth quoting:

'Clean the bird thoroughly and stuff it with the largest onion you can find, first seasoning the onion with salt and pepper and pressing into it a large number of cloves.

'You then take the bird without plucking it and bury it in the ground for at least one month. Dig it up, pluck and truss and cook it in a slow oven for at least five hours, basting it from time to time with its own juice.

'When thoroughly done, remove it from the oven and take out the onion. Throw the capercaillie away.

'Serve the onion with melted butter. Sufficient for one.'

The reason for my father's petulance about the capercaillie was that he had none on his estate, whilst his neighbour who lived further up the glen committed the unforgivable sin of having them in profusion. In fact, properly cooked, capercaillie is a delicious and unusual dish.

One of the most controversial points about cooking game is how long it should be hung. It used to be said that the correct way of dealing with a pheasant was to hang it by the tail until it was sufficiently decomposed to fall to the ground.

It used to be the fashion to eat game very high but this is not now generally the case.

In fact, most game birds in the opinion of many connoisseurs are best eaten on *the day they are shot*, before the muscles contract.

Most game is, however, already several days old before it comes into the hands of the cook and careful attention should be paid to hanging.

Under ideal conditions it is difficult to hang game too long. That great sporting personality, the 5th Earl of Lonsdale, gave his lawyer every year a brace of end-of-season grouse for his birthday. Grouse shooting ends on the 10th December and the lawyer's birthday was on the 15th May, but the birds were always in perfect condition.

The ideal way to hang game is by the beak in an outside larder with metal gauze walls, so that the wind can blow through. This is hardly practical in most cases nowadays but every effort should be made to hang the birds in a cool and preferably draughty place. In any case, birds should not be hung for less than a week to ten days to allow time for the muscles to relax again.

Before giving individual recipes for different species of game bird, here are a few rules which should be observed when cooking all game.

Never pluck a bird until the day it is to be eaten, otherwise it will lose its flavour.

Never, under any circumstances, wash the bird before drawing. This also destroys the flavour.

All game birds should be salted inside before cooking.

Most game cooks like to insert a knob of butter and a couple of spoonfuls of sherry or Madeira inside the birds before cooking.

How to Pluck Poultry and Game

Game birds are always easier to deal with than a chicken because, as they are generally hung for 7–14 days, the feathers come out more readily. Not many people nowadays are faced with plucking chickens, but if you are, pluck them while still warm.

The method of plucking all game birds is quite simple but of course with practice you become more expert. Hold the bird on the table with the left hand and pluck the feathers away from you with the right hand, always pulling away from the root. This way you will avoid tearing the skin. Continue plucking in this manner, using more force for the tail and wing feathers. When completed, singe all over with a lighted match to clear up any straggling feathers. Cut off the head and remove the crop and place the neck in a bowl of cold water to go with the giblets for gravy. Now fold the skin over the neck opening and deal with the inwards. Make a semicircular opening low in the stomach with a sharp knife, just large enough to remove the giblets etc. Place the heart, liver and gizzard in the bowl of water, first removing the spleen from the liver. The spleen is a small bag attached to the liver and if not removed will give a very bitter taste to the gravy.

Wipe the bird inside with a damp cloth. Now tie the bird into a neat parcel with some string, having removed the claws with a pair of kitchen scissors.

The above method is the same for all game birds with the exception of woodcock, plover and snipe which are cooked without gutting.

Sauces for Game

It has always been my contention that to resort to exotic sauces is an admission of failure by the cook to produce something which is in itself appetizing. However, there is no doubt that a really appetizing sauce can add greatly to the enjoyment of your guests but I warn you that it takes time and trouble. Here is a sauce which can add originality to any game or poultry and which I learnt from an old soldier whose father had been a butler in one of Scotland's grandest houses, so I will call it simply Freddy's Game Sauce.

FREDDY'S GAME SAUCE

For venison, game, chicken or turkey. (Ingredients for a large party)

A	**B**
stock	5 apples
tabasco sauce	2 potatoes (just cooked)
black pepper	3 bananas
pimento	glacé cherries (handful)
curry powder	sultanas (good handful)
brown sugar	
water	

Put a large breakfast cupful of stock (venison, game or chicken) into a pudding basin and skin off grease. Then put in a dash of all ingredients marked 'A', but not too much curry powder for game. Do not put in sugar yet. Taste after adding each condiment.

Core, peel and cut into medium sized cubes 3 of the apples and add to the mixture. Put in 2 potatoes (lightly cooked), cut into fair-sized cubes, then bring mixture to the boil, adding another breakfast cupful of stock, seasoned as above. Leave to simmer for 20 minutes.

Boil some brown sugar in a little water. Cut bananas into sections and drop into boiling sugar. When slightly cooked, drain the bananas and drop into the sauce without the sugar. Then cut up the rest of the apples and add. Add sugar to the sauce to taste, including the boiled sugar. Drop in the sultanas and sliced glacé cherries.

Mix a little flour with water to make a thin paste, add some of the hot sauce and then stir the flour mixture into the sauce to thicken. Allow to simmer for a few minutes and serve as hot as possible.

For the sauce addict I also give here a very much more simple one which I have found goes very well with wild duck, woodcock or snipe.

SAUCE FOR WOODCOCK, WILD DUCK OR SNIPE

1 glass of port
2 tablespoons brown
   stock

1 teaspoon red currant
   jelly
a pinch of cayenne or
   tabasco

Put all ingredients into a pan and bring to the boil (i.e. until the jelly melts) and serve as hot as possible.

Pour a little over the bird and serve the rest separately, including juice from the cooked bird.

BREAD SAUCE *(An essential accompaniment of Fowl and Game)*
For six to eight people

1 pint (600 ml) milk
4 ozs (100 g)
   breadcrumbs
1 small onion
4 cloves
6 peppercorns

1 teaspoon salt
Cayenne pepper
1 tablespoon butter
2 tablespoons cream
   (optional)

Simmer the onion stuck with cloves and the peppercorns in the milk for 15–20 minutes. Strain the milk over the breadcrumbs, add seasonings, butter and the cream (if used), and then reheat.

Do not be sparing with the bread sauce.

Pheasant

The pheasant is the most common of all our game birds and also, in the case of the cocks, the most colourfully plumaged. The hens are drab-looking things by comparison. However, if the cock pheasant you see hanging up at your game dealers or sent to you by kind friends does not have the distinctive white collar and brilliant golden feathers to which you are accustomed and is instead dark plumaged, do not turn your nose up at him on that account. These are melanistics – usually a cross with the common pheasant to improve breeding strains – and are equally good eating.

Unlike most game birds, the difference between young and old is not readily distinguishable. With very young cocks shot at the beginning of the season (pheasant shooting starts on 1st October and ends on the 1st February) the spurs may be very much shorter and less 'horny' than in an older bird. By the end of the season many year-old birds, however, have very long spurs indeed and it is no real guide.

For the expert there is one sure test of age. This is by examining the bursa. Hold the bird on its back with the left hand and bend back the tail. This will expose the natural vent and in the case of a young bird (cock or hen) the bursa inside the lip of the vent. In young birds this secondary vent on the side nearest the tail will be easily seen. It only has a depth of about one inch (2½ cm) and gradually closes up as the bird gets older until it disappears altogether, often becoming a slight lump instead.

Even if you do not read the signs right at first try, examining the bursa is a piece of gamesmanship which will certainly impress your game merchant and other know-alls!

Season	1 October – 1 February inclusive
Hanging time	7–14 days.
Size	A cock will feed 5 people, a h'en is smaller and will feed only 4, but it has a better flavour, is more tender and less dry.
Accompaniments	Clear gravy, bread sauce, fried crumbs, game chips. Mushrooms, chestnuts, braised celery, apples and oranges go well with pheasant.
To roast	Season inside and out with salt and pepper. Place a knob of butter inside the bird, smear the outside with a little butter, cover breast with fatty bacon and roast at 400°F, 200°C, Gas Mark 6 for 45 minutes, basting well. Remove bacon 10 minutes before end of cooking time to brown the breast.

PHEASANT IN GIN

1 pheasant	2 tablespoons butter
1 egg	lemon juice
½ cup of breadcrumbs	3 slices bacon
12 juniper berries	½ cup of gin
marjoram	

Lightly beat the egg and stir in the breadcrumbs, juniper berries, a pinch of marjoram and one tablespoon of butter. Stuff the bird with this mixture, and rub caracass all over with butter and lemon juice. Lay fatty strips of bacon across breast, tie up and roast for 45 minutes at 375°F, 190°C, Gas Mark 5. Remove bacon and pour gin over the bird. Cook again for further quarter of an hour or slightly less. Dish up and serve with bacon.

A suitable sauce can be made as follows:
Take the required quantity of red currant jelly, say three large tablespoons, melt gently over heat. Add grated rind and juice of an orange. Serve cold.

CASEROLED PHEASANT

1 pheasant, seasoned &
   dusted with flour
2 oz (50 g) butter or oil
¼ lb (100 g) diced
   cooked ham
salt and pepper

¾ pint (400 ml) stock
¼ lb (100 g) button
   mushrooms
4 tablespoons red currant
   jelly

Prepare the bird and fry on all sides in the melted fat until browned. Put in a casserole, add ham, salt, pepper and stock and cook in moderate oven (350°F, 180°C, Gas Mark 4) for 2 hours. Add whole mushrooms after about 1½ hours and stir in the jelly just before serving.

Grouse

In my not so humble opinion – because I have eaten more game than most people who have not reached my great age – the Red Grouse is the finest of all game birds.

Perhaps I am slightly prejudiced in its favour, because it is our only truly indigenous bird, to be found nowhere else in the world except Scotland and the North of England, but I'll stick to my guns.

Grouse shooting opens on 12 August and finishes on 10 December, although few sportsmen shoot them that late in the season. By that time the rich have departed to warmer climes and it is only the very hardy who will turn out on a wind-blasted moor to pit their wits against such a wily adversary. In the golden summer days they are a fairly easy mark but once the coveys are broken up and there is snow in the wind, it is a good man who can bring them down as they flash over his head at up to eighty miles an hour.

I am often asked if the grouse that appears on the menus of opulent hotels, and even in distant New York, on the evening of the opening day at prices which make a Scotsman's hair stand on end, have really been shot that morning. I believe with the miracle of modern transport that in many cases they have, but there are undoubtedly many mugs who pay good money for a bird which has spent the last nine months in a deep freeze.

There is all the difference in the world in the eating of young birds and old birds. The bursa test of the age of the birds as described for pheasants is accurate, as it is for all game birds, in the case of grouse there is a much easier method. In young birds the primaries or front wing feathers

47

are sharp and pointed whilst the remainder are rounded. In old birds all the feathers are rounded at the tips.

Grouse of more than one year old shed their toenails between the months of July and September. If you have the chance of picking your own birds, look out for broken toenails and reject them!

Grouse do not travel well. Even in those expensive ventilated cardboard boxes, they are apt to overheat. If you are the recipient of a brace of grouse which have been at the mercy of British Rail for some time, I would recommend a tip I picked up from a fellow-Scot, Julia Drysdale, as fine a game cook as I know (see *The Game Cookery Book* published by Collins). Her cure for overheated or rather high birds is simply to dip them in Milton. One would imagine that this would leave them tasting of babies' nappies or something but it does not. It works, but I wonder who on earth thought it up in the first place!

Season	12 August–10 December inclusive. They are best in September.
Hanging time	3–4 days if very young, otherwise 6–7 days.
Size	A young bird will feed two people, an older one three.
Accompaniments	Clear gravy, bread sauce, fried crumbs, game chips, cranberry sauce. Apple and celery salad goes well with grouse.
To roast	Season inside and out with salt and pepper. Place a knob of butter inside the bird, smear the outside with a little butter, cover breast with fatty bacon, place on a piece of toast and roast at 400°F, 200°C, Gas Mark 6 for 20–25 minutes. 10 minutes before the end of cooking time remove the bacon to brown the breast. Serve the bird on the toast.

GROUSE AND MUSHROOMS

1 young grouse
1 lb (450 g) mushrooms
1 oz (25 g) butter

2 tablespoons cream
Salt and pepper

Put about 6 large mushrooms, skinned and cut into quarters, inside the bird. Fry in butter all over, preferably in a casserole. Cut up remainder of mushrooms, skinned, into small pieces, season with salt and pepper, add these to the casserole and fry gently. Add the cream and simmer for ½ an hour. A young grouse should not take longer than ¾ of an hour to cook over all.

JELLIED GROUSE

2–3 old grouse
2 eggs

gelatine
salt and pepper

Take 2 or 3 old grouse, skin them and put on the stove to simmer in enough water to cover. When tender, take all the meat from the bones and cut up finely. Add 2 halved hard-boiled eggs. Reduce the water the birds were boiled in, add salt and pepper and measure. You will probably have about 1 pint (600 ml) stock. Using ½ oz (15 g) of powdered or leaf gelatine to each pint (600 ml) of liquid, soak the gelatine in 3 tablespoons of cold water or cold stock. If using powdered gelatine just stir the soaked mixture into the hot liquid until dissolved. If using leaf gelatine drain and squeeze it before mixing into the hot stock. On no account must the gelatine mixture be allowed to boil. Mix in the grouse and eggs, turn into a suitable dish and leave to set.

Partridge

When I was a boy, the partridge was a much commoner bird in my part of the world than the pheasant. It was a poor day when my brother and I, walking up a few stubble and turnip fields, did not come back with half a dozen brace, and at grown-up shoots they formed by far the greater part of the bag.

That is all changed now. The farmers with their artificial sprays and the cutting down of their hedges have seen to that. More is the pity, for they are fine table birds with a far more delicate flavour than either the grouse or the pheasant. It means that you have to be that much more careful with the cooking than you have to be with other game birds or you'll make a muck of it.

You tell a young partridge from an old one in the same way as a grouse. Pointed primary feathers in the young birds are a sure and quick method, but the legs are also indicative. The young birds have markedly yellow legs whilst the legs of older partridges are much greyer. Age is even more important with partridges. With fine young birds straightforward roasting is hard to beat. With old birds you have to be a bit more guileful.

Season	1 September–1 February inclusive. Best in October and November.
Hanging time	Grey or English Partridge 3–4 days. Red-legged or French Partridge 6–7 days.

Size	One bird will feed two people.
Accompaniments	Clear gravy, bread sauce, fried crumbs, game chips. Watercress and apples and celery salad go well.
To roast young partridge	Season inside and out with salt and pepper. Place a knob of butter inside the bird, smear the outside with a little butter, cover breast with fatty bacon, place on toast and roast in a fairly hot oven (400°F, 200°C, Gas Mark 6) for 25–30 minutes. Remove the bacon towards the end of the cooking time in order to brown the birds.

PARTRIDGE CASSEROLE

Brace of birds
4 onions
2 rashers of bacon
2 tablespoons vegetable
    oil
2 carrots
2 oz (50 g diced bacon

pepper and salt
sprinkling of chopped
    parsley and thyme
1 savoy cabbage
stock made from
    trimmings

Truss the birds and place an onion inside each one and a rasher of bacon over each. Put them in a casserole with oil, sliced carrots, and onions cut into rings, the diced bacon, pepper, salt and the parsley and thyme. Parboil the cabbage, drain it and cut into four. Pack this round the birds in the casserole, barely cover with boiling stock, and simmer gently with lid on for 3 hours. Serve in the casserole.

Sufficient for 4–6 persons.

Wild Duck

I had an uncle who had a bad habit, when serving in India, of going out without his solar topee. The result was that when he came to retire to this country, it was the general opinion that he was 'not quite right in the head'. Once, when I was staying with him, he announced that he was going out to shoot duck. It was not long before he was back, highly delighted with himself, with a couple of brace of Aylesbury duck which had quite evidently been recently swimming on the pond at the home farm.

In fact, he was not so far out, for the domestic duck is the ancestor of the mallard – the most common of our wild duck, and there is very little difference when it comes to the pot.

The main thing to watch with wild duck like mallard, teal, and widgeon is to beware that they have not been shot on tidal waters. If they have, they will have an unpleasant fishy flavour. This can be combated by placing an onion inside them before cooking.

The sure way of telling a young duck from an old one is that in the young, the webbing of the feet can be torn quite easily. Also, their bills tend to be brighter.

Remember that wild duck – even mallard – are smaller than, say, an Aylesbury. Four persons to a mallard is, in my opinion, on the ungenerous side.

Season	In or around the high water mark – 1 September–20 February. Elsewhere – 1 September–31 January. They are best in November and December.
Hanging time	1–3 days.
Size	A wild duck will feed two or three people.
Accompaniments	Clear gravy, redcurrant jelly, watercress or orange salad.
To roast	Season inside and out with salt and pepper. Place a knob of butter inside the bird and smear the outside with butter. Cook in a moderate oven (350°F, 180°C, Gas Mark 4) for ¾ – 1 hour. Baste frequently.

DUCK AND ORANGE CASSEROLE

1 duck, jointed
seasoned flour
½ oz (15 g) lard or
   dripping
¼ lb (100 g) mushrooms

1 oz (25 g) flour
¾ pint (400 ml) stock
¼ pint (150 ml) orange
   juice
1 orange

Coat duck with seasoned flour. Melt fat and fry duck on all sides until brown. Put in casserole. Fry mushrooms lightly and add to casserole. Stir flour into fat and brown over low heat. Gradually add hot stock and orange juice and bring to boil, stir, pour over duck and cook in moderate oven (350°F, 180°C, Gas Mark 4) for 1 hour. Carefully remove rind from orange with potatoe peeler and cut into thin strips. Remove pith and divide orange into segments. Blanche strips of rind in water for 5 minutes and sprinkle over cooked casserole. Garnish with orange segments.

Snipe

Snipe, like woodcock, should be cooked without being cleaned. Indeed, cleaning is hardly necessary as the snipe feeds in marshy places, thrusting its long bill into the ground and drawing sustenance from the mud. It passes through the body so it really has no stomach.

Snipe come in three sizes: the tiny Jack Snipe, the large and comparatively rare Great Snipe, and our indigenous Common Snipe. In the case of the Common and Jack Snipe, I suggest two per person to make a decent course.

Season	12 August–31 January inclusive. Best in October and November.
Hanging time	3 or 4 days.
Plucking and drawing	Do not draw. Skin head and leave it on. Truss, using beak as a skewer passed through the body.
Size	One or two per person.
Accompaniments	Clear gravy, fried potatoes. Garnish with watercress.
To roast	Season with salt and pepper. Brush well with melted butter, cover with bacon and place a knob of butter inside the bird. Stand the bird on a rack with a piece of toast underneath to catch the drippings. Roast in a moderate oven (350°F, 180°C, Gas Mark 4) for 10–15 minutes, basting

frequently. Serve on the toast. Snipe can be grilled under a low grill for about 15 minutes. Timing depends very largely on the taste of your guests. Some like their snipe just 'passed through the flame', others like them well done. However you cook them be sure they are piping hot when served. A half-congealed snipe is most distasteful.

Woodcock

The woodcock is the only bird I know which in moments of danger carries its young to safety. It does this by grasping them between its powerful thighs. People who say this is an old wives' tale don't know what they are talking about. I've seen them do it.

This is only interesting from the cook's point of view, because when the bird is hung, the thigh and leg tendons contract so that unless great care is taken to see that it is carefully hung, it results in a very tough bird indeed. Some shooters get round this by breaking the bird's leg as soon as it is shot. I find this is effective, although it's a pity to spoil a fine table bird.

Remember that one of the pecularities of the woodcock is that it does not need gutting. If your guests are squeamish, don't tell them this. It is apt to put some of them off and you are depriving them of a treat.

All that is required is to take out the gizzard and make sure that you pluck them carefully, for the skin is easily bruised to the detriment of the bird.

I am not a great admirer of the French as game cooks. They may excel in other branches of the culinary arts, which have no place in this book, but they do not know how to cook woodcock. The French will shoot anything from a lark to a blackbird, and the woodcock, which migrates across France in large quantities, is regarded as a special dispensation of Providence. They even have a club of woodcock eaters, The Club National des Bécassiers.

They believe, as I do, that woodcock should be cooked for

a long time so that the full flavour of the inwards should have a chance to permeate the bird.

Here is the way it is cooked by the French experts and in some of the great country houses of Britain.

1 woodcock	sprig of thyme
lard	½ glass white wine
large knob of butter	a little stock
salt and pepper	

Prepare the bird, leaving the head on. Twist the legs to come close to the body and tuck the head and long beak under the wing. Lard thinly all over.

Melt butter in a thick-bottomed saucepan, add woodcock and cook gently for up to 15 minutes. Butter burns very easily, so this must be done with extreme care. Add seasoning and pour over white wine (or champagne, if you are feeling extravagant).

Cover the pan and leave to cook over a very low heat for an hour. Add stock as necessary from time to time but not for a quarter of an hour before removing from the heat. After cooking for some time the contents of the stomach liquefy and leave the body. Scrape out any bits remaining and spread on squares of bread fried in butter. Place the fried bread under the woodcock and serve *piping hot*.

The correct preparation of woodcock is quite easy but it takes time and patience. If the domestic situation does not allow this or if your guests revolt at your cooking the bird – guts and all – try a simpler recipe, like Casserolled Woodcock.

Season	England and Wales – 1 October–31 January Scotland – 1 September–31 January.
Hanging time	About 7 days.

57

Plucking and trussing	Woodcock must be very carefully plucked including the head and neck Do not draw. Twist the legs at the joints to bring the feet on to the thighs. Press the wings to the sides. Put the head under one wing with the beak skewering the body. The legs and breast must have a string tied round them, and also round the head and tip of the bill.
Size	One bird per person.
Accompaniments	Clear gravy. An orange and watercress salad goes well with woodcock.
To roast	Season inside and out with salt and pepper. Place a knob of butter inside the bird and smear the outside well with butter too. Cover breast with fatty bacon, place on a piece of toast and roast for 15–20 minutes at 400°F, 200°C, Gas Mark 6.

CASSEROLLED WOODCOCK

per person:

1 Woodcock
slice fatty bacon

1 tablespoon of butter
slice of bread

Clean the bird. Rub in butter liberally and cover with bacon. Place the birds, however many required, as tightly packed as possible in casserole with tight-fitting lid. Add a little water. Put in a hot oven (400°F, 200°C Gas Mark 6) and cook for 20 minutes. Cut the crust off the bread and fry lightly. On removing the birds from the casserole, pour surplus liquid over fried bread and place a slice under each.

Pigeon

Do not despise the humble woodpigeon. They are cheap and cheerful birds, easy to pluck and easy to cook. Don't bother to hang them, but empty their crops straightaway, as the contents are apt to flavour the flesh.

Personally, I never bother with the wings and legs of pigeon. There is nothing on them and they are more trouble than they are worth. The breast is, however, very satisfying. In pies, casseroles and so on, don't be stingy with the number of birds you use. You can afford them.

Season	All the year round, but best at harvest time.
Hanging time	Unnecessary, they should be eaten very fresh.
Plucking and drawing	Wash and wipe dry. Cut off head, neck and feet at the first joint.
Size	One for two people, or one each.
Accompaniments	Clear gravy, watercress. Red wine, cabbage, cider or apples go well too.
To roast	Young birds can be roasted, older ones are dry and tougher and need more careful cooking. Season bird inside and out with salt and pepper. Place a knob of butter inside the bird and fatty bacon over the breast. Roast in a brisk oven (375°F, 190°C, Gas Mark 5) for 20–30 minutes.

10 minutes before the end of cooking time place a slice of toast under each bird and serve on the toast.

PIGEON FRICASSE

4 pigeons
generous 1 oz (25 g)
   butter or good
   dripping
½ lb (225 g) green peas
¾ pint (400 ml) water

salt and pepper
2 sliced onions
2 crushed cloves garlic
parsley
1 teaspoon wine vinegar
2 egg yolks

Quarter each pigeon and fry them in butter or dripping until light brown. Take some green peas and fry them also till they are bursting. Pour on boiling water and season liquor with pepper, salt, onions, garlic, parsley and vinegar. Cover closely and simmer gently for 35–40 minutes, or until tender. Thicken with yolks of eggs.

JUGGED PIGEON

4 pigeons
2 hard-boiled eggs
sprig of parsley
1 lemon
½ oz (15 g) suet
4 heaped tablespoons
   fresh white
   breadcrumbs
pepper and salt

nutmeg
1 raw egg
1½ oz (35 g) butter
2 sticks celery or a little
   celery salt
bunch of sweet herbs
4 cloves
a little mace
a little flour

Pluck and draw the pigeons, wiping very dry. Boil the livers for a minute or two, and mince finely. Bruise the livers with a spoon and mix with the yolks of the hard-boiled eggs, a sprig of parsley, grated lemon peel, suet, breadcrumbs, pepper, salt and nutmeg. Mix in the raw egg and 1 oz (25 g) butter. Stuff pigeons (including crops) with the mixture, dip them into warm water, dust with pepper and salt and put them into a jar, deep casserole, or earthenware pot, with the celery, or celery salt, sweet herbs, cloves, mace and white wine. Cover jar tightly and set it in a pan of boiling water for 3 hours. When pigeons are done, strain gravy into a stew-pan, stir in knob of butter rolled in flour, cook until thick and pour over pigeons. Garnish with slices of lemon.

POTTED PIGEON

3 pigeons
a dash of Worcester
    sauce, if liked

pepper and salt
a little melted butter

Skin and clean the pigeons. Place them in a pan, cover with water and simmer until the meat is leaving the bones. Remove from the fire and when cool enough to handle, carefully take away all bones and mince meat finely. Put the bones back into the saucepan and boil until the water has been reduced to about 1 cupful. Season and add the Worcester sauce, if liked. Moisten the mince with the stock from bones and a little melted butter. Press into jars, and run a little melted butter on the top to seal each jar.

Capercaillie

In spite of my father's attitude to the Capercaillie mentioned in the introduction to this section, it can be an excellent table bird. The translation of its name from the Gaelic means 'horse of the woods', which does not refer to its culinary shortcomings but to its mating call, which is not unlike the sound made by a galloping horse!

A fully grown caper cock is about the same size as a medium weight turkey and the secret is to cook them for a long time. It is the only game bird which it is difficult to overcook. The flesh is brown on the breast when you first start to carve it but as you cut deeper, it turns almost as white as a chicken. Altogether a very odd bird but don't disown it if one comes your way.

Season	1 October–31 January inclusive. Best in November.
Hanging time	7–14 days.
Plucking and drawing	As for other game (see p. 41).
Size	Will feed 12 people.
Accompaniments	Clear gravy, fried crumbs, game chips, bread sauce. Watercress for garnish.
To roast	Season inside and out with salt and pepper. Stuff with ¼lb (100 g) beefsteak and cover breast with fatty bacon. Roast in a covered pan in a very cool oven (250°F, 130°C, Gas Mark ½) for about 7 hours.

CAPERCAILLIE CASSEROLE

1 capercaillie	1 pint (600 ml) red wine
6 potatoes	1 bay leaf
1 onion stuck with cloves	1 tablespoon seasoning

Wipe the inside of the bird with a clean damp cloth, then put the potatoes inside. These are thrown away when the bird is cooked as they are just for absorbing the pine flavour. Put the onion with cloves in the crop end of the bird and place in a large casserole to which you add the red wine, bay leaf and seasoning. Cook for five to seven hours in a slow oven 250°F, 130°C, Gas Mark ½ depending on the size of the bird – as it is difficult to overcook and I have had a large bird in the oven for as long as eight hours. Add chicken stock if the casserole begins to dry out. When cooked, serve the casserole accompanied by rice or mashed potatoes.

ANOTHER CASSEROLE OF CAPERCAILLIE

1 capercaillie	½ pint (300 ml) game
5 rashers of fat bacon	stock
bacon fat	1 dessertspoon redcurrant
1 pint (600 ml) cream	jelly
giblets	1 tablespoon flour
	seasoning

Draw and truss bird and tie bacon rashers round it. Brown bird in hot fat. Place bird in casserole and pour cream over. Cover and cook slowly on top of the stove, for 2–2½ hours, basting every ½ hour. Cook giblets, omitting gizzard, in stock and remove. Mince liver. Add pan juices, liver and jelly to stock. Mix flour to a thin cream with a little water, add to stock and cook for about 10 minutes. Adjust seasoning. Gravy may be poured over bird, or served separately.

Rabbits and Hare

How to Skin and Paunch Rabbits and Hare

Place the hare on the table and make an incision down the belly with a sharp knife or kitchen scissors. Cut right round the circumference of the animal, making sure you only cut the fur and not the inner skin. You then strip the fur over the back legs and pull the other half of the fur over the front ones. Now cut off the feet at the first joints and remove the head; some people prefer to skin it as well. In this case the eyes are removed with a sharp knife. Wipe the body with a damp cloth but do not wash.

Now slit the stomach lenghwise from the fork of the back legs up to the breastbone. Pick the animal up by the fore legs, give it a quick shake and the guts will fall out on to your kitchen paper. They are held in by one small membrane attached to the top of the backbone and you can cut this with a sharp knife. Leave the kidneys in place but remove the liver, being careful not to puncture the gall bladder which should not be cut out and discarded. Cut the diaphragm and draw out the lungs and heart, but only keep the heart. In the case of the hare all the blood will have collected in a membrane in the thorax and this must be saved in a bowl for cooking later. A little vinegar in the blood will stop it clotting.

Rabbits are cleaned and skinned in the same manner as hares but they may be soaked in salted water for several hours afterwards, which improves both the colour and the flavour.

Rabbits

Anybody who has a prejudice against rabbit since myxo-matosia swept the country is an ass. By all means do not use diseased rabbits, but an uninfected rabbit is easy to recognize and there are plenty of perfectly healthy rabbits to be had.

In my opinion a young rabbit, properly cooked, is a far tastier dish than the average chicken and there are many interesting ways of preparing it.

You can tell a young rabbit from an old by the ease with which its ears can be torn, but, anyway, an old rabbit looks old and grey compared with a sleek young one. Rabbits should always come into the house ready cleaned. No keeper worth his salt will ever carry home an ungutted rabbit. If by chance you get an ungutted one, gut it immediately and complain loudly. A game dealer once told me that he did a big export trade to the Continent in rabbits and his customers insisted that they were sent over uncleaned. What on earth do they do with the guts?

Season	All the year round.
Hanging time	Must be eaten within 3 days.
Size	Will feed 4–6 people depending on size.
Accompaniments	Redcurrant jelly. Good cooked with onions, herbs, bacon or cider.
To roast	May be whitened by soaking in salted water or water with a dash of vinegar overnight or for a couple of hours. For recipe for roast rabbit see page 66.

ROASTED RABBIT

1 rabbit
French mustard

4 slices fat bacon
3 oz (75 g) butter

Take whole rabbit, without head, and smear the outside with French mustard. Then wrap the rabbit all over in thin slices of fat bacon, tying them on with string or cotton. Put the rabbit in a roasting tin, baste it well with butter, cooking it in a moderate oven (350°F, 180°C, Gas Mark 4) for 20 minutes to the lb (450 g).

RABBIT PUDDING WITH MUSHROOMS
For 6 people

2 young rabbits cut up in
   joints
1 tablespoon of chopped
   onion
sage
good plate of mushrooms
few slices of fat bacon

pepper and salt
½ lb (225 g) self-raising
   flour
¼ lb (100 g) good suet
6 tablespoons cold water
   (for suet crust)

Make a suet crust with the flour, suet and cold water. Line a 6"–7" (15 cm–18 cm) pudding basin with ²/₃ of the crust. Put in a layer of rabbit, chopped sage and onion, then a layer of peeled mushrooms, and continue until the basin is filled. Sprinkle plenty of flour between each layer, as that makes good thick gravy. The slices of bacon should be cut up in thin strips and put in each layer with salt and pepper. Add water until the basin is ¾ full. Roll out remaining ¹/₃ of pastry and lay over basin, covering right over the rim. Press well round the edges and trim. Cover pudding with kitchen foil or a double layer of greaseproof paper, pleated across the middle, or a floured tea cloth. Tie securely and set in a steamer or on an upturned saucer in a large saucepan. Half fill saucepan with boiling water and cover tightly with lid. Steam for 3 hours, replenishing with *boiling* water at intervals as necessary. The water will boil away at the rate of about 1 pint (600 ml) an hour. This is a very tasty dish.

BOILED RABBIT

1 young rabbit, cut up in
   joints
salt and pepper
2 large onions

3 oz (75 g) butter
¼ pint (150 ml) double
   cream

Soak rabbit pieces in cold salted water for 2 hours. Put them in a pan with boiling water to cover. Add seasoning. When it boils again, reduce the heat, let it simmer for a good hour and three quarters, and then serve it with the rich onion sauce poured over it. For this, mince or grate the peeled onions, stew them gently over a low heat in butter with a lid on the pan so they melt rather than brown.

After removing the cooked rabbit, boil down the stock violently till it reduces to only about ¾ pint (400 ml) and is full and rich. Stir this into the soft buttery onions.

Add seasoning to taste and lastly, some hot thick cream. I mean cream and not just the top of the milk. Pour sauce over the rabbit. Plain boiled potatoes go very well with this.

RABBIT CASSEROLE WITH MUSHROOMS AND ONIONS

1 young rabbit, cut into
    joints
1 oz (25 g) butter
½ oz (15 g) flour
salt and pepper
1 bay leaf
sprig of parsley
sprig of thyme
½lb (225 g) mushrooms
12 pickling onions or 1
    large onion
strip of lemon peel

1 egg
juice of 1 lemon – or
    dessertspoon of white
    wine vinegar

Soak the rabbit for 2 hours in cold salted water. Dry it. Fry the pieces gently in a little butter without browning. Sprinkle them with flour, add enough water to cover, also some salt and pepper, a bay leaf, sprig of thyme and parsley, mushrooms, the button onions, or some ordinary onion peeled and finely chopped, also a strip of lemon peel, if available.

Let it simmer for 1½–2 hours, depending on the time at your disposal, but the slower and more gently it is cooked the better it will taste.

Just before serving, beat up an egg with the juice of a lemon or with a dessertspoon of white wine vinegar. Add a little hot, but nowhere near boiling, rabbit stock, stirring it gradually into the egg mixture.

Then mix this thickened gravy with the rest of the stock and meat. Serve with plain boiled floury potatoes.

RABBIT FILLETS

1 rabbit	1 egg
salt and pepper	milk
1 sliced onion	salad oil
2 tablespoons flour	

Skin a rabbit and soak it in cold salt water for 12 hours or overnight. Cut meat off the bones in fillets, season with salt, pepper and onions, and let it lie for an hour. Make a batter of 2 tablespoonfuls flour, 1 egg and a little milk. Add 3 drops of salad oil. Dip the fillets of rabbit in the batter and fry in deep fat. Serve with rolls of fried bacon and peas.

RABBIT WITH PRUNES

1 young rabbit	1 oz (25 g) butter
½ pint (300 ml) red wine	½ oz (15 g) plain flour
2 tablespoons wine vinegar	¼ pint (400 ml) stock
1 large onion	½ lb (225 g) prunes
2 carrots	(soaked overnight in cold tea)
faggot of herbs	1 teaspoon redcurrant jelly
2–3 cloves	
6 peppercorns	seasoning

Joint rabbit and marinate overnight in wine, vinegar, sliced onion, carrot, faggot of herbs and spices. Remove rabbit and dry with cloth. Heat butter in heavy pan and brown rabbit pieces. Sprinkle in flour, strain on stock and marinade. Add prunes and redcurrant jelly and season. Simmer gently for about ¾ of an hour or until tender. If, at the end of the cooking time, there is too much liquid it may be poured off and reduced by rapid boilding.

RABBIT STEW

2 rabbits
seasoned flour
¼ lb (125 g) bacon
2 oz (50 g) butter
12 pickling onions or 3
   quartered onions

Approx 1 pint (600 ml)
   stock
faggot of herbs
salt and pepper

Joint the rabbit and coat in seasoned flour. Fry bacon in the butter until crisp, add the onions and cook until lightly browned. Add the rabbit pieces and sauté carefully for half an hour. Pour in enough hot stock to come halfway up the rabbit. Season and add faggot of herbs. Bring up to the boil, cover and simmer for a further 1¼ hours. When cooked, remove rabbit and boil up the sauce once more before straining over the rabbit.

Serve with boiled cabbage and creamed potatoes.

Hare

Hare is much stronger meat than rabbit and generally speaking requires greater care in cooking. The effort is, however, well worthwhile.

Season	There is no season but hare may not be offered for sale between March and July.
Hanging time	10–14 days or longer.
Skinning and Paunching	See introduction to Rabbit section.
Size	A young hare will feed 5 or 6 people. An older animal will feed between 6 and 10. It is wise to stuff a smaller animal with forcemeat to make it go further.
Accompaniments	Thickened gravy, forcemeat balls, red-currant jelly, green vegetables.
To roast	The rather dry flesh of a hare is often greatly improved by marinating before cooking. For roasting it must be brushed with melted fat and very well covered with fat bacon. Cook it in a baking dish with a lid or cover with foil to keep the flesh moist and tender. Cook for 1½–2 hours in a moderate oven (350°F, 180°C, Gas Mark 4).

ROAST HARE

For 6 people

1 young hare
4 oz (125 g) streaky
   bacon
1 pint (600 ml) red wine

seasoning
2 tablespoons redcurrant
   jelly.

Take a young hare and place whole in a roasting tin with the bacon placed over the back. Add the wine, seasoning and redcurrant jelly. Roast in a medium hot oven (375°F, 190°C, Gas Mark 5) for 1½ hours. Serve with the juice from the baking tin as the gravy.

JUGGED HARE

1 hare
a little seasoned flour
faggot of herbs
2 onions (each stuck with
   3 cloves)
½ teaspoon black pepper

strip of lemon peel
2 oz (50 g) butter
2 oz (50 g) flour
2 tablespoons tomato
   ketchup
little port wine, if liked

Retain about ½ a pint of the hare blood. Wash hare and cut into small joints, dusting each piece with a little seasoned flour. Put these in a heavy stew-pan with herbs, onions, cloves, pepper and lemon peel. Cover with hot water and let it simmer until tender, about 2 hours. Take out pieces of hare, lay them in a serving dish and keep hot. Make a roux with the butter and flour and use some of the stock and the blood to make the gravy. Add ketchup, boil for 10 minutes and, just before serving, add the port wine. Strain through a sieve over the hare and serve very hot. Do not omit to serve redcurrent jelly.

HARE IN RED WINE OR CIDER

1 young hare
seasoning
3 carrots
2 small turnips
3 onions
faggot of herbs
bay leaf
12 peppercorns
2 cloves garlic
lemon peel
4 oz (125 g) bacon,
    chopped

approximately 1 pint (600
    ml) red wine or cider
approximately 1 pint
    (600 ml) water
¼ pint (150 ml) sour
    cream or carton of
    yoghourt
1 tablespoon redcurrant
    jelly

Rub the hare with the seasoning and simmer the vegetables (sliced), garlic, peppercorns, lemon peel, herbs and bacon in equal quantities of wine and water. Add the hare and cover with sufficient wine and water to immerse. Simmer in a covered pan or casserole until tender, about 2 hours. Remove the hare and joint it to make it easier for serving. Strain the sauce or put in a liquidizer, if preferred. Blend in the cream or yoghourt and pour over the hare and serve with redcurrant jelly. Sometimes I add the jelly to the sauce and serve the hare with a cranberry or rowan jelly instead.

A SIMPLE HARE STEW

1 hare
3 oz (75 g) bacon
2 tablespoons butter
seasoned flour
1 pint (600 ml) beefstock

1 bay leaf
6 peppercorns
4 small sliced onions
2 large glasses port or red
    wine

Cut the hare into small pieces (approximately 2 in, 5 cm) and the bacon into strips, melt the butter and fry meat and bacon until brown, then transfer to a stewpan. Stir in the seasoned flour, add stock, bay leaf, peppercorns and onions. Cook covered in a slow oven (300°F, 150°C, Gas Mark 2) for about 2½–3 hours. Remove lid and add the wine and continue cooking until it thickens.

Serve with mashed potatoes.

HARE WITH PAPRIKA

saddle of hare
2–3 onions
2 oz (50 g) lard
1 teaspoon salt
1 tablespoon paprika
a little hot water
¼ pint (150 g) sour
    cream

For the dumplings:
½ lb (225 g) flour
½ lb (225 g) suet
¼ teaspoon salt
cold water

Chop the onions and cook in hot fat until golden but not brown. Add the hare cut in thick slices. Season with salt and paprika, and add a little hot water from time to time until meat is quite tender. Stir in the cream and when well mixed, serve with dumplings made as follows:–

Mix flour, shredded suet and salt until it resembles bread-crumbs. Add enough cold water to make a stiff paste. Shape into round dumplings, drop into boiling salted water and boil for ½ hour.

Venison

It is an odd thing but nowadays venison has fallen out of favour with housewives in this country. Indeed, it was never very popular in the south but greatly appreciated by country folk in Scotland.

The main reason for its unpopularity is that the meat is very dark-coloured, rather the colour beef turns when it is going off, so perhaps the attitude of the uninitiated is understandable. Butchers also tend to be wary of selling it, because it is not really a very economic proposition in small cuts.

It is a pity that venison is not appreciated as, properly cooked, it is a delicious dish. Instead, almost all the deer shot in this country is sent to the Continent, where it is regarded as a great delicacy.

The stag is a very much larger beast than the hind, the saddle weighing perhaps 14 lbs, of which only about 15% is bone. The haunch can be anything up to 40 lbs, whereas the hind saddle weighs perhaps 8lbs and the haunch 10–14 lbs. Hind is at its best in November – later on it is apt to be in poorer condition. Stags are in their prime in July or early August. Prime venison should be roasted or stewed, but other cuts can make a very good goulash. The favourite demanded by the French from our exporters is known as *Roti de Bêche* and is shoulder wrapped in a net.

Season   There are some deer in season all the year
round but the close seasons are as follows:

Species	Sex	England & Wales	Scotland
RED	Stags	1 May to 31 July	21 Oct to 30 June
	Hinds	1 Mar to 31 Oct	16 Feb to 20 Oct
FALLOW	Buck	1 May to 31 July	1 May to 31 July
	Doe	1 Mar to 31 Oct	16 Feb to 20 Oct
ROE	Buck	1 Nov to 31 Mar	21 Oct to 30 April
	Doe	1 Mar to 31 Oct	1 Mar to 20 Oct
SIKA	Stags	1 May to 31 July	1 May to 31 July
	Hinds	1 Mar to 31 Oct	16 Feb to 20 Oct

Hanging time   8–14 days.
Size   5–10 lb haunch in a young animal.
Accompaniments Jellies, redcurrant, cranberry. Chestnuts.
To roast   Lard and marinate for 2 or 3 days before
cooking. The leg or saddle are best for
roasting. Smaller pieces may be stewed.
Chops and fillet are suitable for grilling.
For roasting, remove from marinade, dry
thoroughly and cover carefully with fatty
bacon or well buttered paper. Roast in a
pan with a lid or cover with tinfoil, at
350°F, 180°C, Gas Mark 4 for 20 minutes
to the pound. A glass of red wine poured
into the pan is good.

VENISON WITH OXTAIL AND RED WINE

5 lb (2¼ kilos) haunch of
    venison
1 bay leaf

1 oxtail, jointed
6 peppercorns
1 pint (600 ml) red wine

Place the haunch in a large roasting tin, together with the bay leaf, oxtail, peppercorns and wine. Cover with baking foil and put in a moderately hot oven (350°F, 180°C, Gas Mark 4) for 3–4 hours, basting occasionally. The oxtail provides the fat, as venison is inclined to be dry. When cooked, remove the oxtail, which can be used to make a delicious soup, and you now have the venison with a rich gravy. Baked potatoes go very well with this dish.

An alternative method is to marinate the venison in American Cream Soda for two days. This has the effect of breaking down the tough sinews and making the meat very tender. The most likely place to find American Cream Soda is in your local fish and chip shop.

GALANTINE OF VENISON

3 lb (1½ kilos) of the
    thick end of breast of
    venison
½ lb (225 g) cooked
    gammon or bacon
1 lb (450 g) pork sausage
    meat

3 eggs
salt
peppercorns
parsley
thyme
marjoram
½ oz (15 g) gelatine

Bone venison and remove any gristle. Cut gammon into small cubes and mix with sausage meat. Boil eggs and leave till cold. Take the bones from venison and put in saucepan of cold water (3 quarts, 7 litres) with salt, peppercorns, parsley, thyme and marjoram. Bring to boil. Put boned meat on a board, skin downwards, spread over half the sausage meat, then eggs cut in halves, then remainder of sausage meat. Roll and tie in a cloth. Place in boiling stock, leaving bones in the saucepan, as they prevent the roll sticking. Boil gently for 4 hours.

Take out, tighten cloth by rolling it up again and place in a dish with a weight to press it. Leave till cold, then remove cloth, and glaze. Strain liquor from bones and boil rapidly until reduced to a pint (600 ml). Thicken liquor with the gelatine, previously soaked in 2 tablespoons of cold water. Glaze the galantine with this and turn remainder into a basin to set. When set, chop finely and use to decorate round the galantine with bunches of parsley.

Meat

Meat

If you don't know your beef, at least know your butcher. So many butchers nowadays do not take the same pride in their trade as they used to. They buy their meat wholesale and retail it with an indifference to cut and quality which is quite deplorable.

Try, if you can, to find a butcher who buys his beef on the hoof and kills it himself. He will be a knowledgeable man, who relies on his own skill to make a profit. Ask his advice and you won't go far wrong.

In general beef is not what it was when I was a boy and that is not just an old man talking. In those days Aberdeen Angus were the supreme beef cattle, known all over the world, and not far behind came the Duns and the Red Polls. The Angus was a small animal, often slaughtered at 16–18 months, having been fed on good natural pasture in the summer months and the old-fashioned diet of turnips, linseed or cotton cake and a little dry hay in the winter. The result was marketed as 'baby beef'.

Alas, demand between the wars grew to such an extent that farmers looked around for a cross that would produce a bigger and more profitable animal. The popular crosses of Angus with Shorthorns and Herefords increased their weight from about eight to ten hundredweight. They produced good meat, if not so finely grained or richly coloured – points to look for when you are buying.

Now it is the fashion to cross our good British cattle with Continental imports aimed at producing still bigger beasts at the expense of quality. The big French animals are more oxen, bred as beasts of burden rather than for beef and are all muscle and bone. The result of this cross is, to my mind, disastrous. Add to this the practice of feeding beef on a diet of barley, which is often done in England, and you have an end product with which the most skilful cooking can do little. You can always tell barley beef by its almost complete lack of colouring, which is matched by its lack of taste.

All this emphasizes the importance of picking your butcher with care. If the fellow does not know how his meat is bred or fed, there is no way in which you can be sure of getting what you want. Such is the slavish fashion for all things French that some butchers in this country (the finest meat-producing country in the world) even defer to snobbish housewives by giving French names to various cuts. What, for example, is entrecôte but sirloin, boned, trimmed and cut to the required thickness?

If you are lucky enough to get a good piece of beef, do not spoil it by trying to make a fancy sauce. Just follow a few simple rules and let the beef itself do the rest.

General Hints for Cooking Meat

When buying beef, buy as large a joint as you can afford. The larger the joint, the better it cooks. My personal preference is for a 7 or 8 lb rib of beef on the bone with plenty of fat.

Before cooking, rub the joint with cooking fat and seasoning. A note of how to make suitable seasoning is given opposite. Cook as slowly as possible and baste from time to time. As a general rule allow 15 minutes cooking time per pound plus an extra 15 minutes. Cook at 350°F, 180°C, Gas Mark 4.

After removing the joint from the heat, allow to settle for about ten minutes. It is not long enough for the beef to get cold and it allows time for the juices to retreat back in to the meat making carving much easier and, therefore, more economical.

For a leg of lamb I insert a clove of garlic between the bone and the meat and add a sprig of rosemary. Allow 20 minutes to the pound cooking time plus a further 20 minutes. Cook at 375°F, 190°C, Gas Mark 5.

When buying pork, get the butcher to score but not remove the rind. Use plenty of oil and salt to make the 'crackling' crisp. Be sure to cook pork well. Allow 30 minutes to the pound plus 30 minutes extra. Cook for the first half hour at 450°F, 230°C, Gas Mark 8 and then at 350°F, 180°C, Gas Mark 4.

Seasoning	I always keep a jar of seasoning made up in bulk. It is an invaluable cooking aid, particularly with meat. Simply mix well together 2 lbs (1 kilo) salt, ¼ lb (125 g) ground black pepper, ½ oz (15 g) mace, and ¾ oz (20 g) cayenne pepper. Keep for preference in a stone jar with lid.
Gravy	Good gravy is essential for the enjoyment of meat and it is perfectly easy to make.

When your meat is cooked (having been regulary basted), there will be a considerable amount of juice in the roasting pan. Pour off excess fat and add a wine glass of water to the residue. Bring to the boil, stirring with a wooden spoon. Do not strain, as some people do, but leave the bits of meat in it.

If the quantity is not sufficient, add a crumbled beef stock cube and a little more water.

Here are a few variations from the standard roasts which you might like to try.

STEAK, KIDNEY AND MUSHROOM PUDDING

If I see steak and kidney pie on a restaurant menu (why hardly ever pudding, which is much more satisfying?) my heart sinks. It is usually an excuse for serving poor quality meat and so little kidney that it becomes a case of 'hunt the thimble'.

Correctly cooked and with the right ingredients this is one of the finest dishes in our national repertoire.

1½ lb (675 g) finest
   rump steak
¾ lb (350 g) kidney
½ lb (225 g) mushrooms
   (field variety if
   possible)
½ cup flour
salt and pepper
¼ pint (150 ml) good
   beef stock
large glass red wine

For the suet crust:
12 oz (350 g) flour
3 oz (75 g) breadcrumbs
6 oz (175 g) best beef
   suet
½ teaspoon salt

First make your suet paste. Chop the suet finely with a little flour. Mix it in with the other ingredients and add water (about $^1/_3$ pint, 150 ml) until a moderately stiff consistency has been obtained. Mixing should be done lightly with the finger tips. Set on one side.

Using a very sharp knife, cut the steak into thin slices about 4″ × 3″ (10 cm × 7 cm) and season the flour with salt and pepper. Now slice up the kidneys and mushrooms, but not too small and make small parcels, wrapping the steak round them. Dust with the seasoned flour. Roll out $^2/_3$ of the dough and line a 7″ (18 cm) diameter greased pudding basin with it. Work it up with your hands to nearly an inch above the rim of the basin so that when you put the pastry lid on you can roll and pinch it to seal it tight. Carefully place the parcels of steak in the lined basin and pour in the red wine and sufficient beef stock to come ¾ way up the basin. Roll out the remaining ¹/₃ pastry and place it over the top, sealing well. Cover with a double layer of greased greaseproof paper with a 2″ pleat across the top to allow for expansion. Tie firmly and cover with a pudding cloth equally well tied. Place in a steamer or on an up-turned saucer in a large saucepan of boiling water with a well fitting lid. The water should come about halfway up the side of the basin and should never be allowed to boil over the top. Steam, as slowly as possible, for about 4 hours topping up with boiling water from time to time as necessary.

THREE DAY LAMB

If you are a well-organized person who likes to plan your dinner parties well in advance, try this way of cooking a leg of lamb.

6–7 lb (2½–3 kilos) leg
    of lamb (or mutton)
egg cup of dry mustard
egg cup of sugar

egg cup of seasoning (see
    page 83)
milk as required
½ cup of cream

Mix the mustard and the sugar with the seasoning and rub well into the joint, which should not be too fatty. Leave in a cool larder for 24 hours.

Place meat in a deep saucepan and cover completely with milk and leave for another two days, or longer. Strain and thoroughly dry the meat before roasting in the usual way, basting it regularly.

Add cream to the gravy instead of water.

PORK CHOPS IN CIDER

6 pork chops
1 pint (600 ml) cider
   (Woodpecker for
   preference)

1 chopped-up cooking
   apple
seasoning (see page 83)

Season the chops on both sides and grill lightly (approximately five minutes a side).

Put cider into a frying pan with the sliced apples and simmer until the apples are soft and cider is reduced. Now put in the chops and continue to simmer slowly for a further 20 minutes, so that the chops are tender and thoroughly impregnated with the cider mixture.

Serve with apple sauce.

HOW TO BOIL A TONGUE

Cold tongue is a good stand-by, particularly when you have a house full of guests. It can be served on its own, with ham and other meats, or used for sandwiches.

1 ox tongue
½ lb (225 g) carrots

½ small turnip

Chop up the vegetables and boil them with the tongue very slowly for five to six hours.

Remove tongue from water and cut off hard outer skin whilst still hot. Place tongue in a cake tin or similar with an inverted plate and a heavy weight on top.

When cold and well pressed, turn out on a serving dish.

When carving tongue, use a very sharp knife so as to cut it in very thin rounds.

A GOOD WAY OF COOKING VEAL

3½ lb (1½ kilos) boned
    breast of veal
1 teaspoon thyme
juice of ½ lemon
1 pkt stuffing mixture
4 oz (125 g) cooked
    chopped spinach
4 oz (125 g) ham
2 tablespoons parsley
2 oz (50 g) butter
½ pint (300 ml) white
    wine

1 oz (25 g) gelatine
1¼ pints (750 ml)
    chicken stock
1 wineglass Madeira (or
    cooking sherry)
¼ pint (150 ml)
    mayonnaise
½ lb (225 g) carrots
2 green peppers

Rub seasoning, thyme and lemon juice into meat. Mix half the stuffing mixture (which you can buy in a packet) with the spinach and spread over the meat. Mix the other half with chopped ham and parsley and spread over spinach. Now roll the meat up and tie tightly with string, coat with butter, place in roasting pan and roast at 325°F, 170°C, Gas Mark 3 for 1 hour.

Pour white wine over the meat. Cover meat with tinfoil and roast for a further 1½ hours. Remove from heat, allow to cool, wrap in a fresh foil and chill for two hours.

Dissolve the gelatine in some of the stock. Add the rest of the stock, the strained and de-greased pan juices and the Madeira and pour $\frac{1}{3}$ into a shallow dish and allow to set for garnish. Mix the rest of the liquid with the mayonnaise and whisk to a firm consistency.

Untie the veal, pour over mayonnaise sauce and serve with the chopped jelly, carrots and green peppers.

STUFFED STEAK

I do not generally recommend messing around with a good steak, but here is a variation I have tried with some success.

1½ lb (675 g) rump or
    sirloin steak, not less
    than ½ in (1 cm)
    thick
4 oz (125 g) chopped
    ham
4 oz (125 g) chopped
    mushrooms
6 chopped spring onions
1 cup breadcrumbs
1 oz (25 g) butter or oil
    seasoning

Cut a deep pocket in the side of the steak.

Mix up the ham, mushrooms, onions, breadcrumbs and a little seasoning and sauté gently in a pan for ten minutes.

Insert mixture in the pocket of the steak. Rub butter or oil on the steak and season, then cook under the grill.

Curry

Curry

Although I served for many years in India, I do not like, so many Englishmen who have lived there, claim that it is the home of the best curries. Indeed, I would say that quite the contrary is the case. Nor do I subscribe to the view that the hotter the curry the better.

The currying of meat in India derives from the necessity of disguising the fact that the meat is very often rancid. The Indian cattle are ill-fed, and in most places religious beliefs forbid their consumption, and Indian chickens more than often feed on dunghills. They both produce tasteless meat, even if it is fresh – hence the need for ever hotter ingredients.

In my own opinion the best curries in India are made of vegetables and the best Indian cooks are Brahman women, most of whom are vegetarians. Alas, few of them migrate to this country. Most of our Indian restaurants are run by male immigrants from the Sylhet districts in East Pakistan and they do not make the best use of the excellent ingredients available here.

The aim of the curry cook should be to bring out the flavour of his ingredients, not to seek to hide them and this in turn means that the utmost care should be used in selecting the beef or poultry or whatever is planned as the foundation of the dish.

I find that curry is an excellent all-purpose dish, particularly suitable for the sort of occasion when you are not quite sure just how many guests are staying on for 'something to eat' after a drinks party.

One of the delights of a good curry is the number of side

dishes which go with it. They are no trouble to prepare and add greatly to the general enjoyment.

No curry dish is complete without the side dishes and the more the merrier in my opinion. Here are a few suggestions for you to try:

Poppadums, which you buy at your grocer and are essential.

Bombay Duck – dried fish, not a bird!

Dahl – for recipe, see below.

Chutneys, in a variety of 'hotness'.

Hard boiled egg, mashed up with Worcestershire Sauce.

Sliced cucumber with natural yoghurt.

Chopped onion and skinned tomato with vinegar.

Chopped orange with pith and pips removed.

Finely grated cheese.

Chopped banana.

Chopped mango.

Crushed peanuts.

Chopped green and red peppers.

Very finely chopped chillies.

Dessicated coconut. Alternatively, try soaking dessicated coconut in warm water. A cloudy white liquid will result which is delicious poured over the curry.

Some people also serve fried sardines – a matter of taste.

Finally, remember that if you make too much curry, there is no need to worry. Curry is the only dish I know of which tastes better re-heated next day.

Dahl is an excellent accompaniment to curry and is well worth the trouble. You will need:

½ lb (225 g) red lentils	1 sliced onion
teaspoon powdered ginger	1 crushed clove garlic
½ teaspoon turmeric	1 pint (600 ml) water
1 oz (25 g) butter	pinch of salt

Wash the lentils and put them into a pan with all the other ingredients, except butter and salt. Simmer gently until the lentils are soft and all the water has been absorbed. Add salt to taste and stir in the butter.

How to Cook Rice

So many people seem to have difficulty in cooking rice that I make no apology for giving this simple method:

For each pound of Patna rice have four pints of rapidly boiling salted water with a good squeeze of lemon juice which keeps the rice a good colour. When you have added the rice, stir for a few seconds with a fork to make sure the rice does not stick to the bottom of the pan. When boiling, cook rapidly for 10 minutes – no more. Then rinse with hot or cold water through a sieve and place in a shallow dish. The rice can then be dried in a slow oven or left and used later for an accompaniment – heating it up again by pouring boiling water over and draining through a sieve.

My Own Curry

This is my standard recipe, which I have used over the years in all manner of situations and which I have found to be very widely appreciated.

2½ lb (1 kilo) chuck
   steak
4–6 tablespoons cooking
   oil
2 large onions
tablespoon cumin seed
tablespoon coriander seed
dessertspoon cardamon
   seed
tablespoon turmeric
crushed garlic

dessertspoon crushed
   chillies
dessertspoon curry
   powder
2 cloves
1 tablespoon flour
salt and pepper
small tin tomatoes
cube chicken stock

Cut steak into cubes about 1½"–2" (4cm–5cm) square.

Heat 3 or 4 tablespoons oil in a fireproof stewpan and gently cook the onion for a few minutes. Grind the cumin seed, coriander and cardamon in a pestle and mortar and add to the onion with the powdered turmeric, garlic, chillies, curry powder and cloves and cook until all the oil has been absorbed.

Heat two tablespoons of oil in a frying pan, add the meat, sprinkle with flour and salt and pepper and fry until lightly brown.

Transfer to the stewpan containing the onion and add the tin of tomatoes and the stock cube, diluted with sufficient water to come ¾ of the way up the meat. Cover tightly and place in a moderate oven (350°F, 180°C, Gas Mark 4) for 1½ hours.

ANOTHER MEAT CURRY

(For 6 people)

1½ lb (675 g) stewing
    beef (shoulder or
    hough will do)
sultanas
3 onions
2 tablespoons curry
    powder

1 small tin tomato purée
salt – be careful as
    tomato purée is
    salted!
coconut juice, (optional)
rice

Trim fat from meat, cut into small pieces and wash. Put into saucepan with handful of sultanas and enough water to cover. Bring to the boil and simmer for 10 minutes. Chop up two onions and add to meat.

Meanwhile heat a little fat in frying pan. Add one chopped onion and cook till golden. Then add 2 tablespoons of curry powder, cook gently for a minute or two and stir the mixture into the meat. Simmer all together for 10 minutes. Add tomato puree and a little salt and put into a stewpan. Cover and cook slowly in oven for about 2½ hours (250°F, 130°C, Gas Mark ½). If available the juice of a fresh coconut may be added about 20 minutes before serving.

Serve with boiled rice to which has been added sultanas.

KOFTA (or KOAFTAH) CURRY

1½ lb (675 g) minced beef
1 large onion, chopped
4 ground cloves
1 egg
1 teaspoon ground cinnamon
1 dessertspoon ground cardamoms
2 green chillies, finely chopped
salt and pepper
2 potatoes, boiled and well mashed
cooking fat

Mix the minced beef and onion in a bowl with the ground cloves, raw egg, cinnamon, cardamoms, green chillies, a little salt and a sprinkling of black pepper. Add the potatoes and mix very well. Lightly flour your hands and mould the mixture into balls about the size of a small apple. Fry them in cooking fat until lightly brown. Drain fat. Now to make a sauce. You will need:

1 teaspoon ground coriander seed
½ teaspoon ground chillies
½ teaspoon ground ginger
½ teaspoon ground turmeric
½ teaspoon cummin seed
cup of coconut milk (or dessicated coconut)
1 tablespoon lemon juice

Mix the spices with a cupful of coconut milk (made with dessicated coconut if desired), a large pinch of salt and the lemon juice. Simmer all together for five minutes.

Place meat balls in the resultant sauce and simmer gently for ½ hour, shaking pan occasionally to ensure they do not stick.

Serve with boiled rice.

CHICKEN CURRY

1 4 lb (2 kilo) chicken, jointed
2 sliced onions
3 chopped cloves of garlic
3 tablespoons cooking oil
2 tablespoons curry powder
¼ lb (125 g) mushrooms
1 chopped apple
½ pint (300 ml) chicken stock
salt and pepper
1 carton natural yoghurt
1 dessert spoon lemon juice

Fry the onions and garlic in the oil until soft. Add the chicken pieces and fry to lightly brown. Stir in the curry powder and cook gently for a couple of minutes. Add the mushrooms, apple and enough stock to form a thick gravy. Cover and simmer until chicken is cooked, approximately ¾–1 hour. Season to taste and at the last minute add yoghurt and lemon juice.

A QUICK CURRY FROM LEFT-OVERS

1–1½ lb (450 g–675 g)
    any left-over meat,
    such as beef, lamb,
    venison or poultry.
1 onion, chopped
2 tablespoons cooking oil
1 tablespoon curry
    powder

1 tablespoon curry paste
1 dessert spoon flour
1 pint (600 ml) stock
1 sliced cooking apple
2 oz (50 g) raisins or
    sultanas
1 tablespoon chutney
salt and pepper

Soften the onion in the oil, add curry powder, curry paste and flour and cook gently for a couple of minutes. Carefully blend in the hot stock. Add chopped meat, apple, raisins, chutney and salt and pepper to taste and simmer for a further 20 minutes.

SWEETBREAD CURRY

1 lb (450 g) blanched and
    skinned sweetbreads
3 sliced onions
1 clove chopped garlic
¼ lb (100 g) butter
1 heaped tablespoon
    curry powder

salt and pepper
6 tomatoes
1 tablespoon lime juice
1 large teaspoon
    cornflour
generous dash of curaçao

Fry the sliced onions and chopped garlic in butter until golden brown. Add curry powder, and salt to taste. Stir well and add three sliced tomatoes. Simmer for five minutes and now add sliced sweetbreads and lime juice. Cover and cook gently for 40 minutes.

Add three more sliced tomatoes and simmer for a further

five minutes, thickening the liquid with cornflour which has been previously mixed with a little cold water.

Just before serving add a dash of curaçao.

TUNA FISH AND EGG CURRY

6 hard-boiled eggs
1 can tuna fish
a little milk
French mustard

For the sauce:
1½ oz (35 g) butter
2 chopped onions
crushed clove garlic
1 tablespoon curry
    powder
1 dessertspoon flour
¾ pint (600 ml) stock

1 large chopped apple
½ lb (225 g) sliced
    tomatoes
2 tablespoons sultanas
1 tablespoon lemon juice
salt and pepper

For the sauce, melt the butter in a pan, add the onions and garlic and cook gently until soft. Stir in the curry powder and flour and cook for a further two minutes. Blend in the hot stock, bring to the boil and simmer for five minutes. Add all the other ingredients and cook gently together for seven minutes more.

Take the six hard-boiled eggs, the flaked tuna fish, a little milk and some French mustard. Slice the eggs lengthwise and remove the yolks. Pound the yolks with the tuna fish, milk and mustard to bind. Fill the egg-white cases with the mixture and sandwich together.

Arrange in a warmed dish and pour the sauce over them.

Curry

Cover the dish with foil and heat in the oven 350°F, 180°C, Gas Mark 4, for ten minutes.

Serve with chutney and sliced bananas sprinkled with lemon juice.

Wine

Wine Notes

When I was a boy, wine on the whole was drunk mostly by the upper classes. Every big house had a large wine cellar, which was a veritable Aladdin's cave, with bins of slowly maturing Port, racks upon racks of clarets and burgundies, ancient Madeiras and fresh clean hocks. The French champagne houses manufactured their brands particularly for the English taste and this country was their largest market. The Master of the house kept his cellar book as meticulously as he did his game book and much time and thought was given not only to the re-stocking of the cellar but to ensuring that the wines were only drunk when they had reached exactly the correct point in their development.

Nowadays the demand for wine is so great that the finest French vintages are being drunk far too young and the days when a fond father could afford to put down a pipe of Port for his new-born son, not to be bottled until the lucky young man came of age, are long since past.

Nonetheless the picture is not altogether black. The widening of the market has brought many wines on to the market which would not have earned cellar room not so many years ago, but which are perfectly palatable and can be drunk every day without ruining the family exchequer. Personally, I find that if one is going to buy a cheap table wine, one does better with the wines of Italy, Spain, Portugal and Yugoslavia, or in fact almost any country except France. On the other hand, in the more expensive bracket the wines of France are second to none.

I should like to put a word in here for Major-General Sir

Guy Salisbury-Jones who has devoted his retirement to cul-
tivating vines at Hambledon in Hampshire, from which he
makes a variety of wines which will stand up in any com-
pany. I believe he has even exported them to France on
occasions.

There is more drivel talked and written about wine in this
country than about almost any subject with the exception of
politics. I will always listen with respect to the views of
people who have served a long apprenticeship in the wine
trade, but so many writers today have little or no qualification
to inflict their views on the public. Nowhere in this more
evident than in the perpetuating of certain 'rules' in wine
drinking which are quoted and re-quoted as if they were a
gospel instead of merely guidelines.

One of the most often quoted dicta is that red wine should
be drunk with meat and white wine with fish. Utter bunkum!
If you are a white wine lover, you can enjoy it equally with
a steak as with anything else, and who shall tell me that it is
not done to drink my favourite claret with a Dover sole? The
only judge of what goes with what is your own stomach.
To my mind, it would be unwise to drink red wine with
shell fish, such as lobster or oysters – but each man to his
taste.

Another aspect of wine drinking which is set about with
snobbery concerns the way it should be served.

Most 'experts' will tell you that red wine should be served
at room temperature, but what on earth does this mean?
Judging by some of the dining-rooms I have eaten in you
might just as usefully put ice in it. The important thing about
serving red wine is to open the bottle an hour or two before
drinking so that it gets a chance to breathe. Even a wine that
is slightly 'corky' will often recover if it is allowed time to
do so. Set the wine in a warm place but be careful not to
overheat. The wine should be just slightly warm to the palate.
The more delicate the wine, the greater the care required to
get it just right. As for the rougher wines, I personally see
nothing very wrong with plunging the bottle into hot water

for a few minutes, if it has to be served at short notice. White wines should, of course, be served cold, but not so heavily iced in the refrigerator as to deprive them entirely of taste. Champagne, in particular, should not be served too cold. I find the practice of plunging the bottle in a bucket of ice to be admirable only if it is not left there too long. Ten minutes is ample.

Much to be deplored is the practice adopted by wine waiters of wrapping a napkin round the bottle, thus effectively obscuring the label. The useful purpose the napkin serves of avoiding drips on the tablecloth can be equally well achieved with a twist of tissue paper round the neck.

It is pretentious to decant cheap wines. Pour them into a wide-mouthed water jug and set it in the middle of the table for people to help themselves. Decanting of the more mature red wines should be done carefully to avoid getting any sediment in the decanter. This is particularly so in the case of old Port. It used to be the custom to illuminate the neck of the bottle by placing a candle beneath it whilst pouring so that any sediment could be detected at the earliest possible moment.

The use of wine in cooking can often turn a pedestrian dish into something rather special, but again there are pitfalls for the unwary. I once heard a chap complain that the wine in which a dish had been cooked was non-vintage. Surely the ultimate in wine snobbery! Of course the fellow, as might be expected, did not know what he was talking about. In general, wine used in cooking should be the roughest available. The more delicate the wine, the less effective.

In my opinion it is well worth keeping a bottle of Madeira for the kitchen. It is much overlooked, nowadays, as a wine for drinking either at mid-morning with a dry biscuit, or an aperitif before a meal (Sercial is the best for this purpose), or as a substitute for port or brandy after dinner (Malmsey), but all types of Madeira are superbly pervasive wines to cook with.

Possibly the best wine of all as a cooking aid is, surprisingly, champagne – and particularly old, flat champagne which is no use for drinking. If you have a friendly wine merchant, ask him if he has any 'ullaged' champagne. This is wine which has gone 'over the hill' and which has wasted away so that the contents of the bottle have shrunk an inch or two. If you can lay your hands on this, you will have the perfect wine for cooking.

Puddings

Puddings

Puddings were, up to the beginning of The Great War, regarded as the crowning achievement of any meal and the
yardstick by which the hostess's culinary skill was judged.
For this reason puddings were very often not left to the cook
but prepared by the lady of the house herself to jealously
guarded recipes.

Alas, puddings are now rather disregarded, except in the
very grandest households. I remember staying in a great
house in Northern Ireland not so very many years ago, where
there was not one but two cooks on the establishment. During my stay one of the cooks was replaced. The first dinner
was perfection up to the pudding stage, when there occurred
a long and awkward pause. When our hostess called impa-
tiently for an explanation, the butler explained, with much
shuffling of feet, that the two cooks had had a disagreement.
The new cook, who had been imported from Southern Ireland, had insisted on producing a confection in the colours
of Mire. Indignantly, the Northern Ireland cook had replied
with an even more magnificent production in red, white and
blue. Tempers had flared and resulted in the two contestants
scraping their puddings out of their hair. We went pudding-
less that night, but I felt satisfaction in the reflection that
pride in puddings had not altogether died out.

The advantage to the dinner party cook, if she goes to the
trouble of creating an interesting pudding, is that it can be
prepared well in advance and not interfere with the preparation of the rest of the meal.

TRIFLE

8 small sponge cakes
2 macaroons (optional)
½ cup of brandy
1 cup Madeira or sherry
1 oz (25 g) walnuts or
    almonds
rind of 1 lemon
2 tablespoons jam

custard
1 cup double cream
1 oz (25 g) sugar
1 egg white
1 tablespoon brandy &
    Madeira (mixed)
glacé cherries

Trifle is, and should be, a rich pudding. Do not be sparing with your ingredients. It is a pudding you can experiment with, putting in more of the ingredients you like and less of those you don't, until you hit on the ideal combination.

Line a glass dish with split sponge cakes or a mixture of sponge cakes and macaroons. Mix half a cupful of brandy with a good cupful of, ideally, Madeira. If sherry is used instead, I have generally found that the cheaper the sherry the better it is for cooking. Soak the sponge in the mixed sherry and brandy till it is saturated. Scatter nuts and grated lemon rind over the sponge and spread with a good layer of jam.

Make some fresh custard in the quantity required (see page 120), according to the size of the trifle, and pour over the trifle when the custard has cooled.

Now whip together a cupful of cream, about an ounce of sugar, an egg white, and a dash of the mixed spirits. Whip until bulk is nearly doubled and heap on top of the dish. Decorate with glacé cherries or anything similar to hand.

QUEEN OF PUDDINGS

1 pint (600 ml) milk
½ lb (225 g)
   breadcrumbs
2 ozs (50 g) butter or
   margarine
grated rind of 2 lemons

2 ozs (50 g) granulated
   sugar
2 eggs
3 tablespoons jam
2–4 ozs (50–100 g) castor
   sugar

Heat the milk and add to it the breadcrumbs, fat, lemon rind and granulated sugar. Leave to soak for 30 minutes. Separate the eggs and stir in the yolks. Pour the mixture into a buttered pie-dish and bake in a moderate oven (350°F, 180°C, Gas Mark 4) until set – about ¾ of an hour. When the pudding is set, spread the jam on top. Whip the egg whites very stiffly, add 1 oz (25 g) of castor sugar and whip again until stiff; then lightly fold in the rest of the sugar. Spread over the pudding, put into a very cool oven (250°F, 130°C, Gas Mark ½) until the meringue is set and golden brown, (about 1½ hours).

BANANA DISH

6 bananas
1 cup red wine
chopped nuts

1 egg
½ cup castor sugar
a little cinnamon

Bring red wine and sugar to boil and simmer for 3 minutes. Remove from stove and add beaten egg and mix well (whisking). Dip bananas in cooled sauce, then roll in nuts. Sprinkle with the cinnamon and pour over remaining sauce.

PRINCE OF WALES PUDDING

1 lb (450 g) cooking
   apples
¼ lb (100 g) sugar
¼ lb (100 g) butter
4 eggs

1 tablespoon flour
3 tablespoons single
   cream
1 lemon
6 oz (175 g) puff pastry

Stew one pound of apples with a little of the sugar and rub through a sieve.

Beat together the butter and the rest of the sugar until creamy.

Separate the whites and yolks of the eggs and beat separately until very light.

Mix the flour with the cream and the juice of one lemon.

Mix all ingredients together, folding in the whites of eggs last. Line a pudding basin with puff pastry. Pour in the pudding and bake in a moderate oven (360°F, 180°C, Gas Mark 4) for about ½ hour, until risen and nicely browned on top.

UNCLE TOM'S PUDDING

½ lb (225 g) treacle
½ lb (225 g) flour
¼ lb (100 g) minced beef
   suet
2 oz (50 g) brown sugar
1 teaspoon ground ginger
1 teaspoon ground
   cinnamon

1 teaspoon ground
   allspice
1 teaspoon bicarbonate of
   soda
2 eggs
teacup of buttermilk

Heat treacle in a basin (either in the oven or over a saucepan of boiling water) and mix in the dry ingredients. Beat up the eggs with the buttermilk and stir into the flour and treacle mixture. Mix well, pour into a buttered mould, tie securely with a double layer of pleated greaseproof paper and a pudding cloth, and boil for two hours.

Serve with egg sauce (page 121).

APRICOT SOUFFLE

2 oz (50 g) butter
2 oz (50 g) flour
2 oz (50 g) castor sugar
tin of apricots

1 tablespoon chopped
    almonds
3 eggs (separated)

Melt the butter in a saucepan. Stir in the flour and sugar and add ½ pint of syrup from a tin of apricots. Stir over fire until boiling, remove from heat and add the almonds (roughly cut), 2 tablespoons of cut up apricots and the 3 egg yolks. Fold in the stiffly beaten egg whites and turn into a soufflé dish. Bake in a fairly hot oven (400°F, 200°C, Gas Mark 6) for 20 minutes to ½ hour.

SYLLABUB

For 4 people

1 lemon
4 oz (125 g) wine, sherry
   or fruit juice
2 tablespoons brandy

2 oz (50 g) castor sugar
½ pint (300 ml) double
   cream

Put thinly pared rind of the lemon and its juice into a bowl with the wine and brandy, and leave overnight. Strain into a deep bowl, add and dissolve sugar. Pour in cream and whisk till ready – not too stiff.

APPLE DUMPLING

6 cooking apples, sliced
2 tablespoons sugar
8 cloves

For suet pastry:
6–8 oz (175–225 g) suet
1 lb (450 g) flour
1 teaspoon salt
2 teaspoons baking
   powder
cold water

To make the pastry, skin, shred and chop suet finely and add to the flour, then add the salt and baking powder. Mix with a little cold water to an elastic dough and roll out on a floured board.

Line a basin with the pastry, fill with the fruit, cloves and sugar. Cover the basin with a pastry lid and put on a cover of greased paper; if boiling it must also be tied in a pudding cloth. Boil or steam for 3–3½ hours. (See page 84).

It is an improvement to sprinkle demerara sugar in the greased basin before lining it with the pastry.

114

APPLE CRUMBLE

1 lb (450 g) cooking
   apples
3 oz (75 g) sugar
teacupful of cake or
   biscuit crumbs
rind of ½ lemon
a little water

For the pastry:
3 oz (75 g) flour
3 oz (75 g) cornflour
2 oz (50 g) castor sugar
½ teaspoon mixed spice
pinch of salt
2 oz (50 g) butter
yolk of an egg

Put the apples in a saucepan with sugar, lemon and a little water. Stew until the apples are reduced to a pulp. Turn out to cool. To make the pastry: sieve all the dry ingredients and rub in the butter until as fine as breadcrumbs. Bind together with the egg yolk beaten with a little water. Do not make the pastry too soft. Knead this until free from cracks and roll out thinly.

Grease a tart ring, line it with pastry, sprinkle half the crumbs at the bottom, fill up with the apple mixture, and cover with the rest of the crumbs. Roll out the remainder of the pastry and cover, wetting edges in the usual way. Bake in a moderate oven (350°F, 180°C, Gas Mark 4) for about ½ hour. Sprinkle with sugar. It is delicious with cold custard. (see page 120).

HONEYCOMB PUDDING

½ oz (1 rounded
   tablespoon) gelatine
1 pint milk

3 ozs (75 g) castor sugar
3 eggs
1 lemon

Soak gelatine in milk for 2 hours, then add sugar, yolks of eggs, well-beaten, and grated rind of lemon. Gently strain this into a small pan and allow to boil for 3 minutes. Meanwhile, beat the egg whites and add them and lemon juice to the mixture. Stir but do not boil. Pour into wetted mould. Cool.

GINGERBREAD PUDDING

6 ozs (175 g)
   breadcrumbs
2 ozs (50 g) flour
a little sugar
6 ozs (175 g) suet,
   chopped very fine

½ teaspoon baking
   powder
1 teaspoonful ground
   ginger

Mix all the ingredients together and steam for two hours in a greased pudding basin. (See page 84). Turn out and decorate with preserved ginger.

Serve with a thin custard. (See page 120).

SYRUP TART

6 oz (175 g) shortcrust
   pastry
3–4 tablespoons golden
   syrup

2 oz (50 g) breadcrumbs
juice of 1 lemon

Line a pie plate with pastry and decorate the edges. Mix syrup, crumbs and lemon juice and spread over the pastry. Bake in a hot oven (450°F, 230°C, Gas Mark 8) for 20–25 minutes.

To make jam tart, divide pastry into sections with thin strips of rolled pastry and fill alternate sections with two different coloured jams. Bake as above.

BANANA AND RHUBARB PIE

1 lb (450 g) rhubarb
grated rind of ½ a lemon
3 oz (75 g) sugar
4 bananas

2 tablespoons castor
   sugar
1 egg white, lightly
   beaten
2 oz (50 g) almonds

Wash the rhubarb and cut into small lengths, put into a pie dish and sprinkle with lemon rind and sugar. Peel the bananas, crush and beat to a pulp with the castor sugar. When soft, beat in the white of the egg, and continue beating until quite stiff. Spread on the top of rhubarb to form a crust, sprinkle the top with blanched almonds, and bake in a moderate oven (350°F, 180°C, Gas Mark 4) for ½ hour.

Serve with custard (see page 120) or cream.

MILITARY PUDDING

(This was a favourite pudding in my days in the Army)

3 oz (75 g) butter
3 oz (75 g) castor sugar
2 eggs
pinch of salt
3 oz (75 g) cake crumbs

3 tablespoons raspberry
    jam
pinch of bicarbonate of
    soda

Beat butter and sugar to a smooth consistency and then stir in the eggs. Add salt and beat. Stir in cake crumbs, jam and add the bicarbonate, previously dissolved in a little hot water. Mix again. Pour into a pudding basin, cover with a double thickness of greased greaseproof paper and steam for 2 hours. (See page 84).
Serve with egg sauce (page 121).

GOOSEBERRY TART

1 lb (450 g) gooseberries
¼ lb (100–125 g) sugar
2 tablespoons water
lemon essence or juice
1 egg
1 oz (25 g) castor sugar

For the pastry:
6 oz (175 g) flour
1½ oz (35 g) butter
1½ oz (35 g) vegetable
    oil
3 tablespoons cold water

Top and tail gooseberries, put in a saucepan with the sugar and water and cook gently until soft. Mash to a pulp, adding a little lemon essence and, when cool, add the beaten yolk of an egg.
Meanwhile, line a sandwich tin with pastry, made from the flour and fats mixed with a little water and rolled out to

about ¼ in (0.5 cm) thick. Pour in gooseberry pulp, and put another round of thinner pastry on top. Make two sharp cuts in the form of a cross in the centre of the tart.

Place in a hot oven (425°F, 220°C, Gas Mark 7) and bake for 20 minutes, until it is a light brown. Finally, whisk the white of egg to a stiff froth and spread over the top of the tart and sprinkle with castor sugar. Put it back in the oven again for 3 minutes. Serve hot or cold.

BREAD AND MIXED FRUIT PUDDING

stale bread	currants
milk	stoned dates
1 or 2 eggs	sugar
sultanas	butter
raisins	

Stale bread, of course, need never be wasted; there are endless ways in which it can be used up. One of the best ways is in a bread pudding, and here is a recipe I can recommend.

Cut some bread into neat dice, put the pieces in a greased pie dish, and pour over sufficient milk just to cover. Leave till soft, then add more cold milk, to which has been added 1 or 2 eggs, according to the size of the pudding, the dried fruit (about 1 oz (50 g) to each slice of bread) and sugar to taste. Stir the mixture very carefully with a fork, being careful not to break the dice. Put a few pieces of butter here and there and bake in a moderate oven (350°F, 180°C, Gas Mark 4) until a golden brown, (about 40 minutes).

119

LEMON FLAN

for the biscuit crust:
7 oz (200 g) crushed
    digestive biscuits
2 oz (50 g) castor sugar
3½ oz (90 g) melted
    butter

for the lemon cream:
¼–½ pint (150–300 ml)
    double cream
the juice and rind of two
    lemons
1 small tin of condensed
    milk

Stir the digestive biscuits and sugar into the melted butter. Press well down around the base and sides of a flan dish and allow to cool. Whip the cream and add the lemon rind and the condensed milk. Whip all this together and mix in the lemon juice. Whip again until thick; pour onto the biscuit crust and allow to set in the refrigerator.

CUSTARD

1 pint (600 ml) milk
2 oz (50 g) sugar

2 oz (50 g) butter
2 oz (50 g) flour
vanilla essence

Heat milk and sugar to boiling point in a saucepan. In a separate saucepan melt the butter, add flour and cook gently, stirring constantly, for a couple of minutes, taking care not to brown the flour. Away from the heat, whisk in the hot milk and sugar. When thoroughly blended return to the heat, bring to the boil and simmer for a further five minutes. Add a few drops of vanilla essence, and serve hot or cold.

EGG SAUCE

1 egg
1 dessertspoonful castor
   sugar

Whisk egg and sugar in a basin over a pan of hot water until creamy.

Specialities of The Mess

Specialities of The Mess

In an Army Mess, with the members often missing main meals through being detained on duty, or hungry young men coming in at odd times wanting something more substantial than a cup of tea and a biscuit, it is useful to have a repertoire of easy to make and tasty dishes which can be knocked up at short notice.

With the hectic, disordered life many of us live nowadays, some of the following suggestions may prove useful to the bachelor cook or the busy housewife.

I have also included a recipe for a Bacon and Bean Casserole, not because it is a quick dish to make but for quite the opposite reason: it can safely cook away slowly all day. If you and the family have a long day's outing, you will not feel like cooking when you get home and you will be glad that all you have to do is take it out of the oven.

SOUFFLE OMELETTE

2 eggs per person

Separate whites and yolks. Beat up yolks, then whisk the whites. Put yolks in pan and as they cook drop whites in and cook as for an ordinary omelette.

BACON AND BEAN CASSEROLE

(Serves 4–5 people)

4 rashers fatty bacon
¼ lb (125 g) cubed
  salami
½ lb (225 g) stewing
  steak, cut in pieces
5 lb (2 kilos) shelled
  broad beans
4 carrots, cut in large
  cubes
2 young turnips, cut in
  large cubes

1 large onion, thinly
  sliced
3–4 tomatoes, skinned
  and sliced
1–2 cloves crushed garlic
stock made from bacon
  bones
pepper

Fry the bacon gently, add salami and meat and fry together in the bacon fat.

Put meat, bacon, salami, prepared vegetables, tomato and garlic into a stew pan and cover with bacon stock. Add pepper to taste. Put on lid and cook in a very slow oven, (250°F, 110°C, Gas Mark ½), for as long as possible, but not less than eight hours. On no account let the casserole boil.

The ideal method of cooking this dish is to put it in the oven early in the morning and leave it there all day until it is required for dinner. Before serving remove fat bacon.

KEDGEREE

1 lb (450 g) smoked
  haddock fillet
1 tablespoon salt
1 lb (450 g) patna rice
3 oz (75 g) butter

4 hard boiled eggs
1 teaspoon cayenne
  pepper
6 slices of lemon

126

Cook the haddock gently in water for 15 minutes. Keep the water in which the haddock has been cooked and put it into a saucepan with more water – 4 pints (2.5 litres) in all – and the salt. Cook the rice in this for 10 minutes only, drain and wash in hot or cold water through a sieve. Take a frying pan and add the butter together with the rice and flaked haddock, stirring gently until warmed through. Place in a shallow dish and put in a slow oven to keep warm. Meanwhile chop the egg whites and sieve the yolks. Add the whites to the fish mixture and use the yolks to decorate the dish.

Season with cayenne pepper and decorate with lemon slices.

Variation: Add 1 tin of anchovies with the smoked haddock.

SMOKED HADDOCK MOUSSE

1 lb (450 g) smoked
    haddock on the bone
½ pint (300 ml) milk
1 small onion, cut in half
a bay leaf
1 oz (25 g) butter
1 oz (25 g) flour
salt and freshly milled
    pepper

1 tablespoon gelatine
¼ pint (150 ml) cold
    water
1 tablespoon lemon juice
¼ pint (150 ml) double
    cream
3 hard-boiled eggs, for
    garnish

Cut the haddock up and put in a saucepan, add the milk, onion and bay leaf and poach, covered, for 10 minutes. Strain, keeping the milk in which the fish has been cooked, and flake the fish finely, reserving for later. Make a white sauce, using the fishy milk, the butter and flour. Add seasoning and flaked fish. Soak the gelatine in the cold water then heat slowly, stirring until dissolved. Remove from heat and add lemon juice. Stir half of this mixture into the smoked haddock mixture, then add 3 tablespoons cold water to remaining gelatine and set both mixtures aside to cool.

Whip cream and fold into haddock and pour into a soufflé dish or 6 small ramekin dishes. Arrange slices of hard-boiled egg on the mousse and when the remaining gelatine is beginning to thicken, spoon over the mixture to cover the mouse and eggs and set aside in the refrigerator to cool.

CHEESE, ONION AND TOMATO FLAN

8 oz (225 g) shortcrust pastry
3 medium-sized onions (skinned and thinly sliced)
a little butter
4 eggs
4 medium-sized tomatoes (skinned and chopped)

8 oz (225 g) cheddar cheese (grated)
dash of Lea & Perrins Worcestershire sauce
pinch of dry mustard
salt and pepper

Roll out pastry and use to line two 7″ (18 cm) flan rings or sandwich tins. To make the filling, fry onions in butter until tender, drain and cool. Beat eggs, add onion, tomatoes, cheese, Lea & Perrins and seasoning. Pour mixture into flan case and bake in fairly hot oven (400°F, 200°C, Gas Mark 6) for 30 minutes. If using flan ring, remove and return flan to oven for a further 10 minutes.

Serve hot or cold.

CAULIFLOWER CHEESE WITH LASAGNE

6 slices of cooked green
   lasagne pasta
¼ lb (125 g) cooked
   mince beef
1 small tin tomatoes
1 small onion, sautéd
1 large or 2 small cooked
   cauliflower

4 hard-boiled eggs
1 pint (600 ml) cheese
   sauce
4 oz (125 g) grated cheese
2 oz (50 g) butter

Line a shallow dish with the pasta, mix the mince, tomatoes and onion together and spread over the pasta. Divide the cauliflower into sprigs and lay over the mixture. Add the halved hard boiled eggs. Cover all with the cheese sauce, dotted with grated cheese and butter and put in a fairly hot oven (400°F, 200°C, Gas Mark 6) for 15 minutes until the top is nicely browned and crisp.

To make the cheese sauce, use the basic white sauce recipe on page 34 and add grated cheddar cheese.

STOVEYS

2 lb (1 kilo) potatoes
2 onions
¼ lb (125 g) dripping

seasoning to taste
(50–150 ml) water

Slice potatoes and put in a pan. Add chopped-up onions, dripping and seasoning and cook gently, adding water occasionally to prevent it sticking, until the potatoes are cooked through. It will take about an hour.

During my army service I found, as I am sure many housewives today will find, that a very valuable stand-by against the unexpected visitor is some form of paté, which can preface the most modest meal and give it just that little bit extra.

Oddly enough, one of the most appalling private soldiers I was ever unfortunate enough to command was a certain Private Proudfoot who, but for his skill in producing a quite excellent, although comparatively simple paté, would have been in almost permanent residence in the Guardroom.

Here it is:

PRIVATE PROUDFOOT'S PATE

½ lb (225 g) chicken
  livers
2 oz (50 g) butter
1 large onion
1 clove of garlic
2 rashers of bacon

tomato purée
salt and pepper
bay leaves
cayenne pepper
knob of butter

Melt butter in pan, add chopped onion, garlic and bacon and cook gently until onion is soft and golden. Add livers and cook for 5 minutes with pan covered. Put this mixture into liquidizer with a teaspoon of tomatoe purée and a shake of salt and pepper. Liquidize until mixture has reached desired consistency and then place in a nice earthenware pot, putting bay leaves on top of the paté. Melt a large knob of butter with a large shake of cayenne pepper and pour over paté and leave to cool.

Sandwiches, too, are a great stand-by but it is extraordinary how unappetizing some people can make them. You are either a good sandwich maker or you are not. Here are a couple of unusual ideas:

LAHORE SANDWICHES

Make a curry paste and add to the remains of cooked chicken, rabbit or white-fleshed game and spread between thin slices of buttered toast.

butter	salt
curry powder or paste	grated cheese
lemon juice	toast
a little chutney, apricot jam or redcurrant jelly	

Carefully blend soft butter and curry powder or curry paste in the quantities required, always a very individual taste. Add a few drops of lemon juice and a little chutney, apricot jam or reducrrant jelly, depending on what meat you are going to use. Add salt to taste. Then, either blend in a liquidizer with the meat, or chop the meat very finely and stir into the curry mixture. Spread between thin slices of buttered toast, cut in squares and sprinkle freely with grated cheese. Heat in the oven for about 10 minutes and dish up on a napkin.

PILCHARD SANDWICHES

1 tin pilchards	anchovy paste or sauce
black pepper	a little tabasco sauce
small amount of cayenne	1½ teaspoons pimento
pepper	

Thoroughly bone the pilchards and rub lightly over a sieve to extract excess oil. Mash in a basin and mix in rest of ingredients, tasting carefully to ensure that no flavour is too strong. Spread on buttered bread. This can be stored in small pots covered with greaseproof paper for use as a standby.

SCRAMBLED EGGS

(for four persons)

Some people think that all you have to do to scramble eggs is to break them into a pan and give them a quick stir. Take a little more trouble and you have a delicious dish instead of a pedestrian one.

6 eggs	½ cupful double cream
6 slices decrusted bread	1 teaspoon
7 tablespoons of butter	Worcestershire Sauce
salt and pepper	

Toast the bread, butter whilst hot and set on edge until needed. Also put out warmed plates. In the final stages of making good scrambled eggs, you have to move fast so that they do not dry in the pan.

Melt half the butter in a thick-bottomed saucepan and then put in the eggs, well beaten together with salt and pepper. Cook over a very low heat, stirring all the time with a wooden spoon. Add thin slices of the remaining butter, piece by piece, taking care that the eggs do not begin to 'set' until all the butter has been melted. If there is any danger of this happening, remove immediately from the heat until they cool slightly. Now allow eggs to begin to thicken. As soon as this happens, pour in all the cream and stir vigorously and shake in a few drops of Worcestershire Sauce.

As the mixture begins to thicken, remove from the flame, still stirring, so that the eggs finish cooking in the heat from the pan. Pour over the buttered toast and serve at once.

HAM AND CHEESE SOUFFLE

(for 6 people)

5 oz (150 g) cooked ham, chopped or diced
3 oz (75 g) grated cheese
6 standard eggs

1 pint (600 ml) savoury white sauce (with added parsley and chives. This can be either bought or home made)

Butter a large soufflé dish, about 4 pints (2½ litres) capacity. Make the savoury sauce and allow it to cool slightly, then stir in the diced ham and grated cheese. Meanwhile, separate the eggs and beat the yolks singly into the sauce. Whisk the egg whites in a mixing bowl until they are quite stiff. Fold the egg whites into the soufflé mixture, using a metal spoon and taking care not to over-beat. Pour into the prepared soufflé dish. Stand the dish in a pan or baking tray of hot water and cook in the centre of a pre-heated oven (350°F, 180°C, Gas Mark 4) for 45–50 minutes, or until golden brown and well risen. You can always add a little grated cheese or breadcrumbs to the top of the soufflé before cooking, which gives a pleasant appearance and a crisp texture.

POTATO SAVOURY

1½ lb (675 g) potatoes	1 tablespoon salt
2 oz (50 g) good dripping	2 Oxo cubes

Boil the potatoes in salted water until tender. Mash with the dripping, crumble the Oxo cubes and mix all together until combined. Grease a pie dish and add potato mixture. Dot with more dripping and place in a fairly hot oven (400°F, Gas Mark 6) until crisp and brown – about 20 minutes.

This was a favourite end-of-holiday supper for the children before returning to school.

GIRDLE SCONES

1 lb (450 g) flour
½ oz (15 g) baking
   powder
pinch salt

a little sugar
a walnut–sized piece of
   butter
a little milk

Mix all the ingredients to a stiff dough with the milk. Handle as little as possible. Cut out into shapes required and cook on girdle until golden brown.

Index

Index

Index